Twentieth Century
LEFTON CHINA
Dinnerware & Accessories

Karen Barton

4880 Lower Valley Road, Atglen, PA 19310 USA

Dedication

Writing a book is in a small way like raising a child. You watch it grow and take shape, guiding it along the various stages of maturity, all the while hoping when you're through, the time, effort, dedication, and love you have put into it will have produced something that was the best it could be ... something you were proud to call yours.

This book is dedicated with love to my sons, Scott and Brian. They are my greatest source of pride.

Copyright © 2005 by Karen Barton
Library of Congress Control Number: 2005928490

Designed by John P. Cheek
Cover design by Bruce Waters
Type set in Zapf Humanist Dm BT/Souvenir Lt BT

ISBN: 0-7643-2281-8
Printed in China
1 2 3 4

Published by Schiffer Publishing Ltd.
4880 Lower Valley Road
Atglen, PA 19310
Phone: (610) 593-1777; Fax: (610) 593-2002
E-mail: Info@schifferbooks.com

For the largest selection of fine reference books on this and related subjects, please visit our web site at
www.schifferbooks.com
We are always looking for people to write books on new and related subjects. If you have an idea for a book please contact us at the above address.

This book may be purchased from the publisher.
Include $3.95 for shipping.
Please try your bookstore first.
You may write for a free catalog.

In Europe, Schiffer books are distributed by
Bushwood Books
6 Marksbury Ave.
Kew Gardens
Surrey TW9 4JF England
Phone: 44 (0) 20 8392-8585;
Fax: 44 (0) 20 8392-9876
E-mail: info@bushwoodbooks.co.uk
Free postage in the U.K., Europe; air mail at cost.

Contents

Acknowledgments and Thanks

At the top of my list of people to thank for making this book possible is Mr. Chester Szaro. He began working for the Geo. Z. Lefton Co. in 1964 as a sales rep, and became manager of their Boston showroom, located in Swampscott, Massachusetts. I am thankful that he kept every catalogue he ever got since he started working for Lefton, because I have them all now and they are an invaluable source of information. Without them this book would not have been possible.

A big thank you goes to Mr. John Lefton, who is Geo. Z. Lefton's nephew. John began working for the Geo. Z. Lefton Co. in the early 1960s. He started working in the warehouse, and over the years worked his way up the ladder, learning every aspect of the business. He is currently CEO of the new Lefton Company, and the last Lefton still associated with the business. I was able to meet John and the see the new Lefton offices and showroom in the spring of 2003. John was generous with his time, patiently answering all the many questions I had about the early years of the company. We still keep in contact and he is still patiently answering questions for me.

I want to thank Marika Berman for the information she gave me over the years about Lefton. Mari began working for Lefton in the mid-1950s as a freelance designer. She was hired as Lefton's full time in-house designer in 1963, and continued working for Lefton until 1990. We have her to thank for designing the Dutch Girl, Hot Poppy, Mushroom Forest, Early American Rooster, and Rustic Daisy dinnerware patterns.

I would like to acknowledge and thank two of Lefton's long time em-ployees for letting me interview them. Both were able to give me valuable info on Lefton's early years. Mr. Sidney Lebow started working for Lefton in 1955 and worked for Lefton for over forty-two years. He was manager and buyer in the New York office. He was able to answer many of the questions I had about Lefton in the 1950s. Also, Mr. Otto Fuarth, who started working for Lefton in 1951. He worked in the Chicago office and was the financial advisor until the company was sold. He knew Mr. Lefton from Hungary, and was able to tell me about what Mr. Lefton sold prior to importing Japanese porcelain after the war.

I would like to give a loving thank you to my husband, John, who photographed all the pictures in this book. He has always been supportive of the long hours I spend working on my Lefton projects, and his patience and help made the long process of writing and editing my books so much easier.

Last, but definitely not least, a special thank you goes to Stuart Brown. I greatly appreciate the long hours he spent checking his Lefton files and catalogues for information I had either missed or entered incorrectly in my files. He was a big help in making this book as complete and accurate as possible. His extensive collection of Lefton items and Lefton catalogues puts him at the top of my list of pre-1975 Lefton experts.

Introduction

Writing this book wasn't something I had planned on doing. It, like my other book, is a result of my many hours compiling Lefton information for myself.

As I acquired my first Lefton catalogues (one or two at a time), I would immediately put the information into an easily referenced computer file, breaking down the information into categories. I kept up with the information as it became available with each newly acquired catalogue. However, when I got four boxes of Lefton catalogues shipped to me by Chester Szaro, the task became overwhelming. It would take every minute of my spare time for the rest of my life to compile all that information ... if I lived long enough! It was then that I decided to take one "line" at a time and compile all the information available in each line. I naturally started with one of the lines I collect, which also happens to be the line most people ask me about ... the dinnerware line.

It is difficult for a collector to know if their dinnerware line is complete, as Lefton made more items in some dinnerware lines than in others. Lefton also made several tea/coffee sets, which just consisted of the pot and the sugar & creamer. And, Lefton made cups & saucers in hundreds of different patterns, but most did not have any other matching dinnerware piece. With this in mind, I limited my "DIN-NERWARE" file to those dinnerware patterns that have at least five pieces in them.

This book contains every item in every dinnerware "set" listed in every Lefton catalogue from 1953 through the rest of the twentieth century. It also contains the only known pre-1953 dinnerware line which is an unnamed fruit pattern. According to information found on the last page of the 1987 Lefton catalogue, this fruit pattern "was produced in 1946." It is believed to be the very first dinnerware set Lefton ever sold. I have an extensive Lefton dinnerware collection, including many "made in Occupied Japan" cups & saucers. I have found lemon plates to match a few of these cups & saucers marked "made in Occupied Japan," but no other dinnerware items.

The pre-1954 items in my collection consist mainly of figurines, planters, vases, cups & saucers, cigarette items, and assorted decorative dishes and accent pieces. This leads me to believe that with the exception of the fruit line produced in 1946, Lefton did not sell dinnerware sets (consisting of five or more pieces) until the mid-1950s. If this is true, then the list of Lefton dinnerware patterns found in this book is complete.

Author's Note

Besides collecting Lefton items, I also collect the Lefton catalogues. I am fortunate to currently have 126 different Lefton "yearly" and "specialty" catalogues in my collection, dating from 1955 to 2003. This is the most extensive and complete Lefton catalogue collection known to exist. I acquired these catalogues from stores that sold Lefton, through e-bay auctions, through long time Lefton salesmen, and through John Lefton. When I told John I had all the catalogues except for one, he sent the last catalogue I needed to make my yearly collection complete.

In addition to these catalogues, there are three other Lefton catalogues known to exist. They are black and white and date from 1953-1954. They are in the possession of Stuart Brown, who also collects Lefton catalogues. He is the only other known person who has an extensive Lefton catalogue collection, although with a few exceptions, his collection ends at 1975 when his interest in Lefton items stops. It has been fun discussing the information found in these pre-1976 Lefton catalogues with Stuart. Except for the 1961 "20th Anniversary" catalogue, the catalogues were not dated until 1964. We worked together to correctly identify the year of each undated catalog by comparing the information found in the catalogues. If a catalogue did not have items found in the other catalogues, we knew it was published earlier. The increased number of Lefton show rooms printed on the catalogue covers also helped us determine which catalogues were printed first. This helped us to assign more correct dates to the Lefton hallmarks & labels.

The information on the Lefton items found in this book comes from the Lefton catalogues. This book contains the most accurate information on Lefton to date, and is as accurate as the Lefton catalogs. According to John Lefton, "our catalog information is what we take as the gospel" ... something accepted as unquestionably true!

NOTE: I was able to get additional information on items not found in the catalogues from early Lefton ads found in *Giftwares* and *Gift and Art Buyer* magazines from the 1950s.

Pricing

You will find two prices after each item listed in this book. The first price is the original price as listed in the Lefton catalogues. The price of an item may have gone up over the years as it continued to be offered for sale, but I have only listed the original listing price. The second price is the current book value. By book value, I mean the price the piece should sell for in a normal market if the object were in mint condition. As with anything, prices fluctuate depending upon the economy or the trends of the day.

I used four sources in establishing the current book value. My first source of reference was the extensive price guide section found in my first book *Twentieth Century Lefton China & Collectibles*. It contains company identification numbers, descriptions, and most current prices for more than 7600 different Lefton items. My second source is the antique stores. Since my husband has retired, we have driven our RV extensively throughout the United States, and we stop at every antique store we pass. I have discovered that prices in the antique stores vary from state to state and as with anything, prices are higher closer to the big cities. I have also discovered that antique store prices are generally higher than e-bay prices, which is my third source for determining a book value. With e-bay reaching so many people all over the world now, I believe that it is the most accurate source for pricing.

Some people are addicted to coffee; I am addicted to the Lefton e-bay auctions. I am on-line almost every day checking out what items are for sale and what they are selling for. I have seen Lefton items go for much less than I think they're worth, but that's usually because the seller didn't include enough identifying information, or identified an item incorrectly, and potential bidders missed finding the auction.

(Not everyone has or wants to spend the time it takes to pull up each individual Lefton auction like I do.) And, I've seen Lefton items go for much more than I think they are worth, which is usually because the bidder didn't know it's value, or got carried away with the bidding excitement, or got into a bidding war with another bidder who was also willing to pay whatever it took to get that last piece needed to complete a collection. For the most part, however, the e-bay prices on items are pretty consistent from auction to auction, with only slight ups & downs in prices.

The fourth source for determining the book value is the Lefton catalogues. I now know the original price of each item, and how long each item was offered for sale. Those items that sold out the quickest in the catalogues and were not reproduced I've priced higher than those items that were offered for sale for a longer period of time. This told me that they either weren't good sellers, or there was a large quantity of those items made.

Lefton History

According to information found on the internet, and information from my interviews with early Lefton employees, the Geo. Zoltan Lefton Company was a multi-million dollar family business that was the producer and importer of giftware, tabletop, decorative accessories, and collectibles for over sixty years.

The original Lefton company was founded in 1941 by George Zoltan Lefton. Mr. Lefton was a native of Hungary, where he worked in his family business designing and manufacturing sportswear. As a hobby, he collected fine porcelains. In 1939 he left Hungary and set sail for America. After arriving in Chicago, Mr. Lefton turned his passion for fine porcelains into a ceramics business, starting out with only three salesmen and fifty SKU's (stock-keeping units).

Little is known about the Lefton pieces that were marketed and sold between 1941 and 1945, although my references state that Universal Statues made products for Mr. Lefton to sell domestically. We do know that no Japanese made items were sold during that time because of the trade restrictions the United States imposed on Japan in 1939.

At the conclusion of World War II, Mr. Lefton traveled to Occupied Japan, where he was able to seal an agreement that revived Japan's porcelain crafting. This was made possible with the help of his Japanese-American friend, Mr. Kanji Nunome. In late 1946, the first Lefton china product with a "Made in Occupied Japan" understamp reached Americans. His success importing giftware from the Orient soon earned Mr. Lefton the unofficial name of "The China King." An ad in the May 1946 issue of the *Gift & Art Buyer Magazine* shows the business being located at 15-131 Merchandise Mart, Chicago, Illinois.

Until the mid-1970s, the majority of Lefton pieces were made in Japan. At that time circumstances regarding Lefton's sources for manufacturing changed, causing Lefton to seek factories and suppliers from other Oriental locations. Although some of Lefton's pieces show they were made in Italy and England, the majority of pieces made during the last quarter of the twentieth century were made in China, Malaysia, Sri Lanka, Korea, and Taiwan, as well as Japan.

From the small warehouse operation grew corporate headquarters that were based near downtown Chicago. Lefton had over 130 representative service accounts in the United States, Canada, and Mexico, and opened show rooms all over the United States. The majority of Lefton's customers were "mom and pop" specialty shops, plus multi-store operations, specialty chains, and those special markets requiring customized products.

After Mr. Geo. Zoltan Lefton passed away on May 29, 1996, his wife, Magda Lefton, became president of the company, and a long time Lefton employee, Mr. John Lefton (George's nephew), became general manager. When Mrs. Magda Lefton passed away in 1998, control of the company went to Mr. Geo. Lefton's daughter, Margo, and her son, Steve Lefton Sharp. Shortly after they took control, Mr. John Lefton left the company. The company was sold in February 2002 to the DEM Holding Company, who had previously been in the gift industry. It was renamed the Lefton Company. The new owner moved the corporate office and show room, which was located for years on Morgan Street in Chicago, to Berkley, Illinois, located near O'Hare airport. The new owner has rehired Mr. John Lefton as CEO and they plan to continue running the company as it has been run for the past 60+ years.

Lefton Designer, Marika Berman

Prior to the mid-1950s, Lefton sold copies of European antiques and "off the shelf" items designed by Japanese artists who worked for various manufacturers. By the mid-1950s, the Geo. Zoltan Lefton Company had grown large enough for them to hire their own artist and designer.

Marianne Berman, known professionally by her childhood nick-name "Marika," was born in Budapest, Hungary, where she had studied since the age of twelve at the famous graphic art school of Almos Jaschik. In 1948 she came to the United States and attended the Cleveland Institute of Art where she received an Illustration Major. In addition, she got a great education while she earned tuition money by designing, sculpting, and decorating items for her uncle, Leslie Berk, who owned a giftware and ceramics business in Cleveland, Ohio. After his business closed, Leslie Berk, who was a friend of Geo. Z. Lefton in Hungary, was hired as the manager for Lefton's East Coast showroom in New York City. Shortly after that, Marika, who also knew Mr. Lefton in Hungary, was hired on a part-time basis to design items for the Geo. Z. Lefton Co. In 1963, she was hired full-time and was their only United States based staff designer until she left the company in 1990.

Some of Marika's early designs are the popular Candy Kane Kids and other Candy Kane theme Christmas items, the Dutch Girl line, Bloomer Girl items, Hummel look figurines, and many of the Angel of the Month series. She later designed the Dollhouse Originals, Marika's Originals, Honey Bears, Pony Tail Girls, Bow Girls, Bloomer Girls, Cupie Cupid Line, Professional and Sports Kewpies, Kewpies of the Month, Piano Babies, Retirement Banks, many of the Month Doll series, most of the Character and Professional figurines, musical figurines, piggy banks, baby items, and almost all of the holiday novelty items. The house ware lines she created for Lefton include Bossie the Cow, Rustic Daisy, Poppy, and Mushroom Forest, just to name a few. She was responsible for the Christopher Collection figurines and musicals, and her "Christopher" designed face is still used today. Under the name "Bryan Wood" she designed the Colonial Village line, including the small figurines in the village. The Colonial Village logo still used today is Marika's design.

The process of designing an item began with a request for a type of product. This could be a knock off of a successful item by a competitor, a special order item requested by a customer, an item suggested by a Lefton salesman or buyer, or a replacement piece for a discontinued item. Other times Mr. Lefton would tell her that he needed an item in a certain category within a certain price range, such as "we need a piggy bank to sell for around $24.00 per dozen." Many times Marika was asked to design an item using as reference an antique or fine art piece, or an illustration such as a greeting card, or a picture of competitor's item. When she was asked to design the Lefton version of Dept. 56's Dickens Village, she referenced the buildings in Colonial Williamsburg, adding snow to the roof and foundation plantings, and putting Christmas décor on the houses.

The second step of the process was to make a group of drawings which were basically representations of the future item. Each drawing was close to the actual size and color that the finished item would be. When the drawing got its final approval, it was sent to Japan to Nagoya Boeki Shokai (owned by Mr. Kanji Nunome), which was the export company that put Lefton on the map. Later designs went to the export company run by Mr. Hattori, a retired Nagoya Boeki employee. The people at Nagoya would determine which factory was the best suited and most readily available to produce the item. Marika's drawings were then given to the factory's artist, who produced the working drawings for the sculptor. These working drawings were altered versions of Marika's designs, changed slightly so the item model was more compatible to fit the factory's kiln system. Each item has to be put into a container of a given size for casting. If the design was 4 1/2", and the casting container was only large enough to hold an item up to 4", the design was altered to fit the closest sized casting container. To use a much larger container than needed wasted kiln space and casting material, making the item unnecessarily more expensive to produce.

After an item was sculpted, a master mold was made. This was never used for production, but only used to make "production molds" from. These production molds wore out after a couple hundred castings, so production molds would have to be remade several times from the master mold. No more than six sample pieces were ever cast from the master mold and then fired in the blank. When the samples were finished with the casting process, they were given to a master decorator who worked out the production sequence based on the original sketch colors. The design sample was then presented for final approval before going to

full production. If the item was satisfactory in looks and price, a minimum order was placed. The number of pieces ordered varied, depending upon the item, from several hundreds to thousands. The minimum order number went up and up over the years. The design samples cast from the master mold would be sent to the three exclusively Lefton "company showrooms" located in Chicago, Los Angeles, and New York. These show room samples were always just a bit higher in quality than assembly line production items, although Lefton's quality control was extremely good, making production pieces very close to the showroom samples.

Many times Marika provided only the basic items to "house ware" lines, such as cookie jars, canister sets, sugar & creamers, salt & pepper shakers, mugs, and a serving piece or two. If the line turned out to be a good seller, the factory would gradually expand it by designing other items in that line. Lefton had an exclusive on the "Kiji" style coffee pot, teapot, sugar & creamer, salt & pepper, pitcher & bowls, etc. You will see identical style items in several of Lefton's patterns, including the Heritage lines, the Chintz lines, Holly Garland, Heirloom (Elegance), Blue Paisley, Paisley Fantasia, Heavenly Rose, Poinsettia (Limited Edition), Yuletide Hollyberry, and Pink Dogwood.

By the way, technically Lefton never produced "dinnerware" with full place settings. None of the lines have soup bowls. This was done for duty purposes so the items would be classified as "giftware" instead of "dinnerware." The U.S. duty on dinnerware was four times higher than on giftware, so the "dinnerware" classification was always avoided. This is one of the reasons why Lefton was so reasonably priced. However, you will be hard pressed to find a soup bowl by Lefton!

Identifying Lefton and Its Age

One of the nice things about collecting Lefton is that, for the most part, it is easily identified. Lefton used three types of identification on their pieces: a fired on hallmark, a paper label, and an identification number.

The identifying mark that people are most familiar with is the Lefton crown. This crown was originally outlined in black and was colored in the middle. It had red lettering around the crown. In the mid-1960s, the colored crown was phased out and a gold crown was used. In the mid- to late 1970s, the crown shape changed slightly, and colored crowns were used again in addition to the gold crowns. Unlike the early crowns where the lettering was a different color than the crown, the lettering on these new hallmarks matched the color of the crown. The majority of hallmarks Lefton used were put under the glaze, and are a permanent form of identification. However, by 1990 Lefton had printed their crown hallmark on plastic labels, and these were attached to many of their items. In addition to the crown hallmark, there were several other hallmarks used. They are pictured in the "Hallmarks & Labels" section of this book.

In addition to the Lefton hallmark, you will find a paper label. The first year paper labels were used to identify the country of origin was in 1954. Until that time, the country of origin had to be under the glaze. The majority of these paper labels were red and gold. Occasionally, however, you will find a Lefton piece with a sticker that is red with silver trim and writing, or a sticker that is black with gold trim and writing. These paper stickers are the least reliable source of identification, as they came off over the years.

The number on the underside of an item is the identifying ordering number, with the exception of a few dated items. Only Lefton knows the exact sequence of their numbering system; however, I have noticed, by looking through the catalogues, that as additional pieces were added to their inventory, the numbers got larger. (There were a few pre-1960 items that had a five digit ordering number, however those are exceptions.) One important discovery I made while looking through my catalogues is the numbering system changed in 1981 and is a way of identifying items made before or after that date. With the exception of those pre-1960 items I mentioned, every Lefton item made before 1981 had a four digit or less identification number. In 1981, every number was converted to a five or more digit number by putting one or more zeros in front of the number. The first item with this new numbering system was #00001, a 4" Footed Mug in the Christmas Holly Pattern. Six digit numbers had a one as the starting number. Knowing this, it is safe to say that all items with a four digit number or less were made before 1981. And, with a few exceptions, all of the items having a five or more digit number were made after 1980.

Lefton Showrooms

Since my husband retired, we have traveled extensively throughout the United States. We stop at every antique store along our way, and I found that certain areas of the United States have more Lefton in their antique stores than others. After looking at the locations of the Lefton showrooms printed on my catalogues, I discovered the reason was because there was a Lefton showroom near those areas.

I believe the most Lefton, and the hardest to find pieces, are located around the Chicago area where the company was based. I go back "home" to that area several times a year to visit family and, of course, hit the antique stores in search of Lefton. I always find something to add to my collection, and a couple years ago I found a real treasure. It is an unusually shaped and patterned chocolate pot (pictured below) and it is not found in any of the Lefton catalogs. I believe it to be either a "special" order item, or a "sample" item that never made it to production. I have never seen another one like it.

Below is a list of the locations of showrooms Lefton had over the years. Some were in existence for only a year or two, while others have been in existence since they opened in the 1950s. I have listed them in the order they appear on the catalogues. The ones with the asterisk after them were the only ones still open at the end of the twentieth century.

Chicago*
New York *
Los Angeles*
Dallas*
Miami
St. Louis
Minneapolis*
Seattle*
Atlanta*
San Francisco*
Nashville
Boston*
Denver
Oklahoma City
Overland Park, KS

Detroit*
Puerto Rico
Columbus*
Portland
Honolulu
Indianapolis
Pittsburgh
Monroeville, PA
Washington, DC
Reston, VA
Kansas City*
Milwaukee
Charlotte
Ontario (1990)
Mexico (1991)
Goldsboro, NC

#3122. Coffee/Chocolate Pot. $350

Hallmarks and Labels

I did not have the 126 different Lefton catalogues I now have in my collection when I wrote my first book, *Twentieth Century Lefton China and Collectibles*; therefore, the information in that book is only as accurate as the research materials used for reference. With these catalogs, I have been able to uncover new information which I am providing here.

A collaborative effort between Stuart Brown and myself was made to find a more accurate version for the dates of the more popular Lefton hallmarks & stickers. In addition to collecting Lefton items, we both collect Lefton catalogues. Between the two of us we have all of the Lefton yearly catalogues from 1955 to 2003. In addition, Stuart has three Lefton undated catalogues which we believe to be from 1953 and 1954. Also, between the two of us, we have more than 3,700 pre-1975 Lefton items, many of which are dated. We spent months examining and comparing our Lefton items with our Lefton catalogues, and compared our findings. The dates given in this book are ones we have been able to verify, and are as accurate as possible based on the information available. There are known Lefton items that can prove a hallmark or label was used past the ending date. We attribute this to the manufacturers using the remaining hallmarks and labels in their inventory before using "newer" marks and labels. These "transition" pieces are an exception to our dates.

Hallmarks
1941-1945

Many Lefton collectors may be wondering why there are no known Lefton hallmarks from 1941 (the year Mr. Lefton started his company) through 1945. The reason for this is because, in 1939, the United States imposed trade restrictions on Japan as a result of the Japanese aggressions in Asia. (You will find nothing from Japan imported between 1939-1945). Little is known about what Mr. Lefton sold during those years. However, on the inside cover page of their 1993 catalogue the Geo. Zoltan Lefton Co. writes "Our first year in business we offered only two items, blue & pink piggy banks, made using a hand dipped glazing process that remains our secret to this day." An ad found in the May 1946 issue of *The Gift & Art Buyer Magazine* shows doorstops and book ends in the shape of puppies that are "life like in detail and color ... these four clever items were molded from prize winning puppies. Material is hard composition with highly glazed natural color China finishes."

All "Occupied Japan" Hallmarks
1946-1952

The Occupied Japan period was from September 2, 1945 to April 28, 1952. Taking into consideration the time needed to design and apply new hallmarks, we have assigned 1946, rather than 1945, as the starting date for all Lefton marks containing the words "Occupied Japan."

Lamore China Entirely Hand Made G.Z.L. U.S.A. Made in Occupied Japan 1946-1952 (Previously dated 1946-1950)

Hand Painted Lefton Made in Occupied Japan 1946-1952 (Previously dated 1946-1950)

Pink Thistle Hallmark
1946-1952

This hallmark is believed to be a manufacturer's hallmark as it is found on items sold by other companies besides Lefton. Below you will find three examples of this hallmark. The Lefton items having this hallmark also had the initials "G.Z.L." on them. Items without these initials were sold by different companies and are not Lefton items.

Hand Painted Made In Occupied Japan G.Z.L.
1946-1952 (Previously dated 1946)

Hand Painted Made in Occupied Japan Endo China
Not a Lefton Hallmark

Hand Painted Made in Occupied Japan
Not a Lefton Hallmark

Samurai Hallmark
1946-1952
(Incorrectly dated 1946-1950)

This is also an example of what is believed to be a manufacturer's hallmark. Again, you will be able to distinguish which are Lefton items by the initials "G.Z.L." Items having this hallmark without these initials were sold by other companies and are not Lefton items. This hallmark is found on items in what is believed to be the first Lefton dinnerware pattern. For more information on this hallmark see the section in this book titled "Lefton's First Dinnerware Pattern."

Tomorrow's GZL Treasures
KOWA Occupied Japan
1952 (Newly Discovered Hallmark)

This is another example of what is believed to be a manufacturer's mark. Since it has the words "Occupied Japan" on it, we know it was used as early as 1952. This hallmark is found on the "Lace Lovelies" figurines pictured on the cover of an undated catalogue, which we believe to be from 1955, judging by the showrooms listed on the cover and the date on an order form found in my copy of this catalogue. These lace figurines were last seen in Lefton's 1956 catalogue. Because of the "Occupied Japan" on this hallmark, it could have been used as early as 1946, however we don't believe it was, as it would mean this item was offered for sale for ten years. Very few of Lefton's items were sold for that length of time. Because the Occupied Japan era ended in 1952, that is the date we have given for this hallmark. The two "Lace Lovelies" figurines we used as reference both had the below hallmark. Research is still being done for the hallmarks that are on the later "Lace Lovelies" figurines made after the Occupied Japan era.

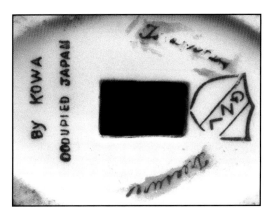

Tomorrow's GZL Treasures Kowa Occupied Japan 1952 (Newly discovered hallmark.)

Hand Painted Exclusively Made In Occupied Japan G.Z.L. U.S.A. 1946-1952 (Previously dated 1946-1950)

GZL Initials
1955-1957
(Newly Discovered Hallmark)

This is another early hallmark discovered by Stuart Brown. While there is no proof that this is a Lefton hallmark, it is a reasonable assumption that it is due to the letters GZL and the rarity in the English language of those three specific letters together. This hallmark was found on a ballerina figurine pictured in the 1956 and 1957 Lefton catalogues. It is the only figurine out of the 3,700+ items used for reference that has this hallmark. It is quite rare and items with this hallmark should be considered collectors items. Since items were generally made the year before they first appeared in a Lefton catalogue, we have given this a starting date of 1955. While it could have been used before or after these dates, we have no proof of that.

GZL Initials
1955-1957 (Newly discovered hallmark.

Lefton China Hand Painted
Made In Japan
1952-1954
(Incorrectly dated 1946-1953)

By law, items made between 1945-1952 had to contain the word "Occupied." This hallmark does not, so we have given it a starting date of 1952. Figurine #968 (baby w/ lace pillow), #953 7" Angel in Tree Figurine, #681 Leaf Shape Dish, all have this hallmark. They are all in an undated catalogue believed to be from 1954.

Lefton China Made In Japan
1952-1954 (Previously dated
1946-1953)

Lefton's Japan
1952-1954
(Incorrectly dated 1948-1953)

This hallmark does not contain the word "Occupied" so we gave it a starting date of 1952. We found three items with this hallmark, two are early head vases, and one is a duck ashtray. These items were all found in the oldest Lefton catalogue that does not list the Lefton-Pacific showroom opened in 1954. This hallmark is rarely seen on Lefton items. Those items that do bear this hallmark should be considered collector's items.

Lefton's Japan
1952-1954 (Previously
dated 1948-1953)

Lefton China Made In Japan
1952-1954
(Incorrectly dated 1946-1953)

The only items we have seen this hallmark on are a pair of cornucopia vases, a swan ashtray, and a lace high-heeled shoe. These items appear in an undated catalogue believed to be from 1954. This hallmark does not have the word "Occupied" so we know it was not used before 1952. It does contain the country of origin under the glaze, so we know that it was used up until 1954. After that time the country of origin did not have to be under the glaze. Given that these items were not found in the 1955 or later catalogues, we feel safe in using an ending date of 1954.

Lefton China Hand Painted Japan
1952-1954

Lefton China
Hand Painted Japan
1952-1954
(Incorrectly dated 1946-1953)

The items we used for reference having this hallmark were also found in what we believe to be the 1955 catalogue. This hallmark does not have the word "Occupied" so we know it wasn't used before 1952. It does contain the country of origin under the glaze, so we know it was used up until 1954. Since items we researched were not found in any later catalogues than 1955, and given that items were probably made the year before they appeared in a catalogue, we feel safe in using an ending date of 1954.

Lefton China Made In Japan 1952-1954 (Previously dated 1946-1953)

Lefton China Hand Painted
(Large Crown)
1954
(Incorrectly dated 1946-1950)

We believe this to be a "transitional" mark. The crown on this hallmark is larger than the smaller crown used between 1954-1956. None of the items in our collection with this hallmark are found in any catalogue after 1954. It does not have the country of origin under the glaze that was mandatory up until 1954 so we know it was not used before that date.

Lefton China Hand Painted (Large Crown) 1954 (Previously dated 1946-1950)

Lefton China Hand Painted
(Small Crown)
1954-1956
(Incorrectly dated 1949-1964)

This hallmark does not have the country of origin under the glaze that was required until 1954, so we know this hallmark was not used before then. We found several dated items in our collections with this hallmark. However, the only dates found on these items were 1955 and 1956. While we found several items dated 1957, they all had the colored crown that also included "Reg. U.S. Pat. Off" on them. We found several items with this hallmark in the 1957 catalogue, but they were first seen in the 1956 catalogue. This information makes us believe that 1956 was the last year this hallmark was used.

Lefton China Hand Painted (Small Crown) 1954-1956 (Previously dated 1949-1964)

© Geo. Z. Lefton
1955-Present
(Incorrectly dated 1950-1957)

The first "Geo. Z. Lefton" hallmark we found was used in 1955. This signature hallmark was used till the end of the century, varying slightly over the years. Without knowing these variations, it will be difficult to accurately date items having only the "signature" hallmark. Luckily, dates were put on many items having this hallmark. Most, if not all, of the 1950s items with this hallmark are found with a date or with a crown mark. Items from the mid-1960s to early 1970s with this hallmark are found without a date and without a crown hallmark. The majority of items made after 1975 with a "signature" hallmark are dated.

© Geo.Z.Lefton –
Dated 1955
1955-Present
(Previously dated
1950-1957)

© Geo.Z.Lefton
– Dated 1970
1955-Present
(Previously dated
1950-1957)

© Geo.Z.Lefton – Dated
1985
1955-Present (Previously dated 1950-1957)

Lefton China Hand Painted
Reg. U.S. Pat. Off
1956-1967
(Incorrectly dated 1949-1964)

Probably the majority of the items used as reference had this hallmark on them. The earliest date seen on this hallmark was 1956, found on item #10566, which is a 6 1/4" Lady figurine (two styles, pink/white) first seen in the 1957 Lefton catalogue, and also item #60329, a hanging wall plate "My Guests Like My Kitchen Best." The "Spring Bouquet" (blue and purple floral) items have this hallmark on them and were first seen in the 1967 catalogue, so we know this hallmark was used until then. We have determined 1965-1967 to be "transition" years, where you will see the ending of the colored crown hallmark used between 1956-1967 and the beginnings of the gold crown hallmarks. Examples of this are "To A Wild Rose" items having a gold crown hallmark and "Festival" items having the colored crown hallmark. Both of these patterns are seen in the 1965 catalogue. The blue floral "Forget-Me-Not" pattern has a gold crown hallmark and "White Pear and Apple" pattern has the colored crown hallmark. Both of these patterns were first seen in the 1966 catalogue. The Limited Edition "Poinsettia" line has a gold crown hallmark, and the blue and purple floral "Spring Bouquet" pattern has the colored crown hallmark. Those patterns were first seen in the 1967 catalogue. What will confuse collectors is the fact that so many items were first introduced with the colored crown hallmark used between 1956-1967, then later re-issued with a gold crown hallmark. The best examples of this are the 1960s bird figurines, and items in the Green Heritage pattern.

Lefton China Hand Painted Reg. U.S. Pat. Off.
1957-1967 (Previously dated 1949-1964)

"L" Below Crown
1963-1969
(Incorrectly dated 1968+)

This is another hallmark that is rarely seen. This hallmark was found on item #1691, an egg box with applied ribbon and flowers. It has a copyright date of 1963 on it. This hallmark is also found on the "Misty Rose" items first seen in the 1969 Lefton catalogue. While this hallmark could have been used in later years, we have found no evidence of that. Because it is rarely seen, we believe it was used only during these years.

"L" Below Crown
1963-1969 (Previously dated 1968+)

Lefton China Hand Painted
Reg. U. S. Pat. Off. (Gold)
1963+
(Incorrectly dated 1955+)

This is one of the two most frequently seen hallmarks, and we had several items to use as reference for dating the beginning of this hallmark. As stated previously, many items produced with this hallmark were first produced with the colored crown hallmark used between 1956 and 1967, so they are not a reliable source for dating. This hallmark was found on items #2319 5 1/2" Butterfly on Flower, #2318 4 1/4" Butterfly on Flower, and #2722 4 1/2" Floral Pieces. These items were last seen in the 1963 Lefton catalogue, so we know that this hallmark was used in 1963. These items were first seen in the 1961 catalogue, so this

Lefton China Hand Painted
Reg. U.S. Pat. Off.
1963+ (Previously dated 1955+)

hallmark could have been used as early as that. However, the colored crown hallmark used between 1956-1967 was also found on these items and it is believed that is the hallmark used on these items before 1963. We did not have enough items in our collections with this hallmark made after 1975 to determine an accurate ending date for this hallmark. We believe that it was phased out in the mid- to late 1970s, when Lefton began using other countries besides Japan to produce their items. At that time, new hallmarks & labels were put on the Lefton items to indicate these new countries of origin.

"L" Below Crossed
Sword & Arrow
1965-1971
(Incorrectly dated 1971+)

This hallmark is not as common as the crown hallmarks and was not used for very long. It is on the underside of figurine #23431 "Woman in Flower Stall" and Figurine #2432 "Man in Book Store." They both appear for the first time in the 1965 Catalogue. This hallmark is found on items in the "Paisley Fantasia" pattern that appears for the first time in 1971. While this hallmark may have been used after 1971, we found no evidence of that.

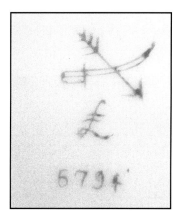

"L" Below Crossed Sword & Arrow
1965-1971 (Previously dated 1971+)

Lefton Bone China
Made In England
1965+
(Previously Undated)

This hallmark is on the underside of a cup & saucer pictured in the 1965 catalogue. No "Made In England" items were found in the pre-1965 catalogues, confirming the beginning date of this hallmark. Lefton has consistently sold English made china from that time to the present. However, most Lefton collectors in the United States seem to be interested in only the "Made In Japan" items, so little effort was spent on researching this hallmark any further.

Lefton Bone China Made In England
1965+ (Previously undated)

Lefton China
Hand Painted (Gold)
1966+
(Incorrectly dated 1955+)

This is one of the most frequently seen hallmarks, and we had several items to use as reference in dating this mark. As stated previously, many items produced with this hallmark were first produced with the colored crown hallmark used between 1956-1967, so they are not a reliable source for dating. The first items we found with this hallmark that are not traced to an earlier hallmark are those in the blue floral "Forget-Me-Not" pattern. This pattern is first seen in the 1966 catalogue. While we do not have a definite ending date for this hallmark, we know it was used as late as 1977 as it is found on items in the "Christmas Tree" w/ presents pattern first seen in that year's catalogue. This hallmark was replaced with one similar to it, except the cross on the newer hallmark is angled to the right.

Lefton China Hand Painted (Gold)
1966+ (Previously dated 1955+)

"L" Above Crown
1967-1977
(Incorrectly dated 1953-1975)

The first use of this hallmark has been traced to the "Character" figurines introduced in 1967. This hallmark is also on the "Tiffany Rose" patterned items introduced in 1977. While the hallmark remains the same, we found this hallmark came in several other colors besides red.

"L" Above Crown
1967-1977 (Previously dated 1953-1975)

Lefton Made Italy
1968-1978 (Previously Undated)

There are several pages of Italian ceramics (called Italian Pottery) in the 1968 catalogue. They continue to be seen in most of the 1970s Lefton catalogues, however the catalogues after 1978 offer for sale those items that were introduced in earlier years. The "Pottery" line was later replaced with Lefton's "Italian Alabaster" line. For those of you who collect Lefton's Italian Glassware, it was first seen offered for sale in an ad in the November 1961 issue of *Giftwares* magazine. It appeared for the first time in a Lefton catalog in 1962. The Italian glass did not of course have a fired on hallmark, but it did have the Italian manufacturer's paper label in many cases. Some examples also had a red Lefton paper label that read, "Lefton's Trademark Exclusives Italy," others a black label that read "Lefton's Made in Italy." Stuart has over 132 Lefton glass items in his collection. The paper label that reads "Lefton Reg. U.S. Pat. Off. Exclusive Japan" appears on glass items appearing in the catalogues from 1962-1973, but was used mainly from 1962-1969. A paper label that reads "Lefton's Japan Hand Blown Glass Works" (a black circular foil) was put on many items from 1966-1974. A surprise was a paper label that reads "Lefton's Taiwan Hand Blown Glass Works" (a black circular foil) that is on items pictured in the 1967 catalogue. Lefton did not sell ceramics made in Taiwan until the mid-1970s.

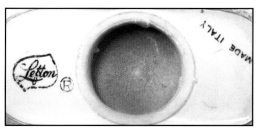

Lefton Made Italy
1968-1978 (Previously undated)

Antique Ivory
Hand Painted By Lefton
1977-1979 (Previously Undated)

"Antique Ivory Bisque" was introduced in 1977. It was offered for sale through 1979. In 1980 it was replaced by the "New White Bisque" line of items. This hallmark is exclusive to the "Antique Ivory Bisque" items.

Antique Ivory Hand Painted By Lefton 1977-1979 (Previously undated)

Christopher Collection
1982-Present
(Previously Undated)

The Christopher Collection was introduced in 1982 with its own specialty catalogue, and it was still being offered for sale in the 2003 Lefton catalogue. Items in this line have a hallmark that says "Christopher Collection" and are dated.

The Christopher Collection © Geo. Z. Lefton 1982 - Present (Previously undated.)

Lefton China Hand Painted
(Angled Cross)
1979+ (Previously undated)

The first appearance of this crown with the cross at an angle is a drawing of it on the back cover of the 1967 Lefton catalogue. Several items that were referenced to find info for this hallmark were pictured in the 1967 through 1975 catalogues. None of those items had this hallmark. Only a few items used for reference were made after 1975. The earliest piece found with this hallmark is a Garden Bouquet dish first pictured in the 1979 catalogue. While this hallmark could have been used as early as 1976, we found no evidence of that.

Lefton China Hand Painted (Angled Cross) 1979+ (Previously undated.)

Lefton Labels

Lefton's Exclusives Japan
1954-1956
(Incorrectly dated 1945-1953)

An article in the October 1955 issue of *Antiques Dealers* states that in 1954 the Bureau of Customs made a ruling that affected the marking of items used since the 1891 McKinley-Taft Tariff Act made it mandatory that all imported ware must be clearly and indelibly marked "under the glaze" as to the country in which the ware was made. The Bureau of Customs made a ruling that "the use of a paper sticker label is a reasonable method of marking imported ware to indicate country of origin." From this information we have concluded that no paper labels identifying the country of origin were used prior to 1954. This explained why we found no labels on any of the "Occupied Japan" items, or those items made before 1954 that we used as reference. This label is commonly seen with the colored "Lefton China Hand Painted" (small crown) hallmark used from 1954-1956. We have not seen this label used with the colored "Lefton China Hand Painted Reg.U.S. Pat. Off." hallmark which began in 1956, so we believe that was the last year this label was used.

Lefton's Exclusives Japan 1954-1956 (Previously dated 1945-1953)

Lefton's Reg. U. S. Pat. Off. Exclusives Japan 1956-1966 (Incorrectly dated 1953-1971)

This label was found on a violin shaped wall pocket #50561, and also a hanging wall plate #60329. Both have a copyright date of 1956 on them. This label was also found on an Oriental figurine w/ lantern numbered 10268, and compote numbered 20053. These items first appear in the 1956 catalogue. This label is on Dutch Blue, Green Orchard, and Pixie Line items that were first seen in the 1966 catalogue. While this label may be found on later items, the use of it much later than 1966 would be unusual.

Lefton's Reg. U.S. Pat. Off. Exclusives 1956-1966 (Previously dated 1953-1971)

Lefton ® Trade Mark Exclusives Japan 1967-1992 (Previously dated 1962-1990)

The earliest item we found that had this label on it was a beaver figurine first seen on the cover of the 1967 Lefton catalogue. This label was also found on cup & saucer #00400 which was dated 1992. This label is frequently seen on items having the "Lefton China Hand Painted" (gold) hallmark, which we believe was first used in 1966, and also the "Lefton China Hand Painted Reg. U.S. Pat. Off" (gold) hallmark, which we believe was first used in 1963 so it could have been used as early as 1963, however we found no evidence of that.

Lefton ® Trade Mark Exclusives Japan 1967-1992 (Previously dated 1962-1990)

Lefton Trade Mark Exclusives Japan 1963-1985 (Incorrectly dated 1960-1983)

Many of the items we found with this label on them were produced over several years, making accurate dating of this label difficult. However, this label was found on a couple of items with the "L below the Crown" hallmark which we have proved was used in 1963. We found no evidence that this label was used as early as 1960. This label was on a baby bootie planter and a pink dogwood bell. Both of these items had the date 1985 on them, proving that this label was used at least until then.

Lefton Trade Mark Exclusives 1963-1985 (Previously dated 1960-1983)

A Lefton Original by Giftcraft 1970 + (Previously Undated)

This label was found on a Mushroom Forest spoon rest dated 1970, and a pair of Orange shaped salt & pepper shakers offered for sale for the first time in 1973. According to John Lefton, Giftcraft was a customer in the 1960s. Since this is not a Lefton label, we did not do extensive research on it. Giftcraft has been one of the leading giftware companies in Canada for over fifty years. Based in Brampton, Canada, just outside of Toronto, they also have permanent showroom facilities in Atlanta and Montreal. Giftcraft is a distributor for their own products as well as those of other companies. You will find almost identical labels as this one on Napco and Enesco items.

A Lefton Original By Giftcraft 1965+ (Previously undated.)

The Lefton - ESD Connection

In 1999 when I began Internet research on my first book, I came across a hallmark that I had never seen on any Lefton item in any antique store. It was a hallmark with the initials ESD. It was on an item that also had the © Geo. Z. Lefton hallmark, so I assumed it was a hard to find Lefton hallmark. Excited about my new find, I started a computerized file on all the items I found with this hallmark. It wasn't long into my research that I discovered only a small percentage of items with this ESD hallmark on them also had the © Geo. Z. Lefton hallmark on them, and I wondered why. Hoping to find an answer, I continued doing research on ESD long after my first Lefton book was published.

To date, I have almost 700 different ESD items in my computerized file. This is a small amount of items compared to the number of Lefton items. My research showed the reason for the small number was because ESD items were only made for about fifteen years beginning around 1955. These 700 or so items were enough, however, to give me some valuable information.

No other Lefton hallmark appears on an ESD marked item except the © Geo. Z. Lefton hallmark. Only a small percentage of items having an ESD hallmark on them also have the © Geo. Z. Lefton hallmark. There are some items that are found with just the ESD hallmark that are also found with just the Lefton hallmark. However, there are hundreds of items found with an ESD hallmark that are not also found with a Lefton hallmark. And, there are thousands of items with a Lefton hallmark that are not also found with an ESD hallmark. There is no Lefton paper label on any item with just an ESD hallmark. There is no ESD paper label (An Enterprise Exclusive Toronto, Canada) on any item with just a Lefton hallmark. The ESD items were only sold in Canada. The Lefton items were only sold in the United States. I began to wonder if in fact these weren't two different companies.

When I met with John Lefton in April 2003, I asked him many questions about the early Lefton years including, "Is ESD the hallmark that Lefton used to sell items in Canada in the mid-1950s-'60s?" His reply was, "Lefton never sold items with an ESD hallmark." (A Lefton showroom was not opened in Canada until 1990 and it was located in Ontario). When I asked him why there are items with an ESD hallmark that also have a Geo. Z. Lefton copyright hallmark, he told me that Geo. Lefton was friends with Harry Pearl, who was the owner of the Canadian company ESD (Enterprise Sales & Distributors 30 Front Street West, Toronto).

In the mid-1950s, when both companies were still growing, the two men would travel to Japan together on their buying trips. By combining their orders, they were able to meet the production minimums required to have an exclusive item. Those items to be shipped to Canada and sold by Mr. Pearl's company had the ESD hallmark put on them. Those items to be shipped to the United States and sold by Mr. Lefton's company had the Lefton hallmark put on them. This is why there are identical pieces with either the ESD hallmark or the Lefton hallmark on them. Each company assigned a different inventory/order number to be put on their pieces. This is why identical items with the different hallmarks also have different numbers.

In the beginning, these were Japanese designed items. Later, as both businesses grew and Lefton was able to hire its own designer, Mr. Pearl continued to sell the Japanese designed items, while Mr. Lefton sold items designed exclusively for him. Occasionally Mr. Lefton would let Mr. Pearl sell some of these Lefton designed items. The ESD hallmark was put on those Lefton designed items along with the © Geo. Z. Lefton hallmark. That is why there are items that have both the ESD hallmark and the Lefton copyright hallmark. A small commission was paid to Mr. Lefton for those ESD/Lefton items when they were sold. By the mid-1960s their business relationship had ended. Lefton continued to grow and ESD eventually went out of business.

NOTE: This is the same relationship the Geo. Zoltan Lefton Co. had with L'Amour China. L'Amour China is also a separate company, and like ESD was based in Canada. While the crown hallmarks are similar, items with the L'Amour China hallmark on them have a paper label common to the ESD label, not the Lefton label. As with ESD, the inventory numbers are different on similar Lefton and L'Amour items. If you look closely, you will notice slight differences in the similar items. For example, the L'Amour "Zodiac Angels" are slightly larger than the Lefton "Zodiac Angels." The L'Amour China Rose Chintz and Violet Chintz snack sets have a different sized cup than the Lefton chintz snack cups. Also, the knobs on the Chintz teapots are different. The L'Amour knobs are square and the Lefton knobs are round.

ESD Hallmark

ESD © Geo. Z. Lefton Hallmark

© Geo. Z. Lefton Hallmark

Lefton & ESD Common Patterns

Below is a list of patterns that can be found with an ESD hallmark and also a Lefton hallmark. Some of these patterns are found with both the ESD and the Geo. Z. Lefton copyright hallmark, but most of them have either one or the other hallmark on them. I have included some pictures of items that are also common to both companies. On items that are too small to have a hallmark on them, you will be able to tell if they are ESD or Lefton by the numbers.

Americana/Regal Rose
Bee Line/Honey Bee
Berry Harvest
Bluebird
Celery Line
Dainty Miss
Daisy Line (Daisytime)
Dutch Girl
Elegant Rose
Elegant Violet
Elegant White
Floral Bouquet
Fruit Basket
Golden Rose
Golden Wheat
Grape Line
Green Holly
Green Orchard
Holly with Touches of Candy Cane Red
Miss Priss
Mr. Toodles
Pear N Apples (Mustard)
Romance
Rustic Daisy
Summertime
Symphony In Fruit
Sweet Violets/Violetta
Yellow Tulip
White Christmas
White Holly

Americana/Regal Rose Plate
#977 Lefton #21148 ESD

Berry Harvest Jam Jar
#299 Lefton #7182 ESD

Blue Bird Salt & Pepper Shakers
#282 Lefton #7182 ESD

Dainty Miss Salt & Pepper Shakers
#429 Lefton #7028 ESD

Dutch Girl Cookie Jar
#2366 Lefton #21865 ESD

Miss Priss Mug
#1503 Lefton #8169 ESD

Fruit Basket Sugar & Creamer
#1667 Lefton #21197 ESD

Summertime Snack Set
#261 Lefton #7214 ESD

Green Holly 6" Plate
#1361 Lefton #7912 ESD

Sweet Violets/Violetta
#2845 Lefton #22193 ESD

Honey Bee Salt & Pepper Shakers
#1288 Lefton #6818 ESD

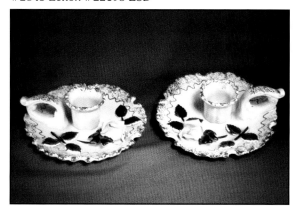

Pink Floral Candleholders
#2149 Lefton #2149 ESD

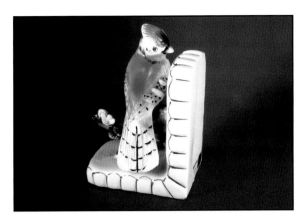

Blue Jay Book Ends
#90581 Lefton #2458 ESD

Bisque Shoe
#1761 Lefton #20422 ESD

Piggy Bank
#379 Lefton #5693 ESD

Graduation Owl Salt & Pepper Shakers
#6826 Lefton #30145 ESD

White Floral Planter
#729 Lefton #5716 ESD

Wall Plate "To Mother"
#508 Lefton #6609 ESD

Mary Mary Quite Contrary
#1107 Lefton #7334 ESD

5" Macaw
#1530 Lefton #21120 ESD

Norman & Elaine
#3045 Lefton #20434 ESD

Planter, Lady w/ Multicolor Dress
#2348 Lefton #21860 ESD

Boy of the Month
#2300 Lefton #25639 ESD

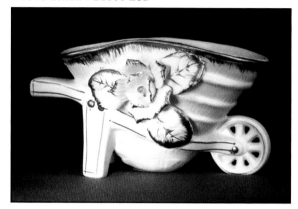

Planter Elegant White
#071 Lefton #7149 ESD

Kewpie Pulling Up Pants
#143 Lefton #7140 ESD

Symphony of Fruit
#1018 Lefton #7728 ESD

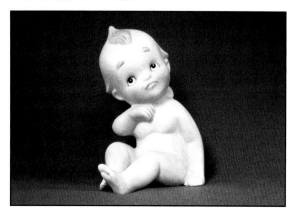

Kewpie Figurine
#913 Lefton #7546 ESD

ESD Girl Head Wall Pocket, Unnumbered

The "Heritage" Lines

Green Heritage is the number one selling Lefton dinnerware pattern. This book would not be complete if I did not include information found only in the Lefton catalogues about this and the other "Heritage" patterns.

The first items in any "Heritage" pattern appeared in the 1956 catalogue. That catalogue contained the #20127 6" Bonbon Dishes in Brown Heritage Fruit & Floral, the #20128 Coasters in Brown Heritage Fruit & Floral, the #20129 Two Tier Tidbit Tray in Brown Heritage Floral, the #20130 Snack Set in the Brown Heritage Floral (and also a possible early version of the Green Heritage pattern), the #20131 Single Tidbit Tray in Brown Heritage Floral, and the #30132 Salt & Pepper Shakers in the Brown Heritage Floral. These items appeared unnamed in the catalogue.

Throughout the years more items in this pattern were made and offered for sale. With the new items also came a new name for this pattern. From 1961 through 1966 Lefton named this pattern the "Heritage Line." From 1967 through 1970 Lefton named this pattern "Floral Heritage." From 1971 through 1972 it appeared in the catalogues nameless. In 1973 through 1975 Lefton named this pattern "Dark Rose Heritage." It was not until 1976 that this pattern was named "Brown Heritage" ... twenty years after first appearing in a Lefton catalogue! Only eight items were offered for sale in 1976. They were #1861, #1863, #1864, #1866, #1867, #1873, #1883, and #2222. Only six items offered for sale in 1976 were offered for sale in 1977. Items #1873 & #2222 were sold out. Only three items were offered for sale in 1978. They were #1861, #1863, and #1883. Other than the musical teapot #7543, no Brown Heritage was offered for sale again until 1985.

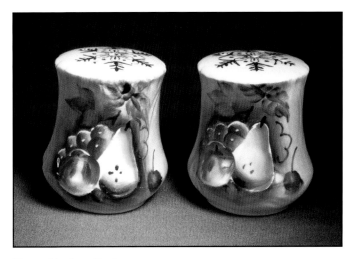

Brown Heritage Fruit
#2760. Salt & Pepper Shakers. $28

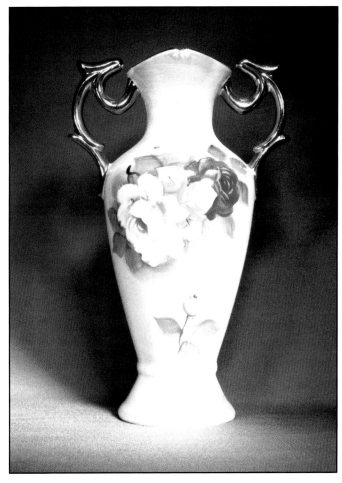

Brown Heritage Floral
#1871. 8 3/4" Vase. $85

The new Brown Heritage floral line (dated 1984) is featured on the cover of the 1985 Lefton catalogue. Only eleven items from this line of Brown Heritage were offered for sale. They were numbered 04149 through 04159. The same items were offered for sale in 1986 with the addition of 04698, the 2 1/2" salt & pepper set. This new line of Brown Heritage was only available for these two years. The only Brown Heritage item offered for sale after 1986 was the 07543 musical teapot. This line of Brown Heritage will definitely be a collector's item.

Brown Heritage Floral – 1985
#04158 9" Plate. $24

Green Heritage (Early Pattern)
#512. Cup & Saucer. $55

There are some patterns that could be considered early versions of the "Green Heritage" floral pattern. As I mentioned on page 29, there is the #20130 Snack Set that had a green background with pink & white roses. In a slightly different pattern, but still with a green background with pink & white roses, is the #510 Coffee Pot, the #511 Sugar & Creamer, the #512 Cup & Saucer, the #513 9" Plate, and the #514 7 1/2" Plate. These were unnamed patterns that are slightly different than the Green Heritage named patterns. Pieces in these two patterns appeared before 1962.

Unlike Brown Heritage, where fruit and floral items appeared in the same catalogue, the first Green Heritage fruit pattern (as it is known by collectors) did not appear until 1965. Only two items appeared in the 1965 catalogue in this pattern. They are the #1860 7" Nappy Dish (three shapes), and the #2720 4 1/2" Candy Box. They also appear in the 1966 catalogue. They are nameless in both catalogues. Nothing appeared in this pattern again until 1971. The items in that catalogue are identical to the Green Heritage floral items except they are in a fruit pattern. They are not called "Green Heritage Fruit" however. They are called "Green Vintage." Items in Green Vintage appear in the 1972 catalogue under the same name, and in the 1973 catalogue nameless. That was the last year this pattern was offered for sale. This pattern is definitely a collector's item.

Green Vintage
#6279. 6 1/2" Pitcher w/ Bowl (Not shown). $225

The first "Green Heritage" pattern appeared in the 1962 Lefton catalogue, and Green Heritage items have been offered for sale every year since then, except for 1998. A paragraph on page 112 of the 1986 Lefton catalogue reads, "That which withstands the test of time, from generation to generation, is truly a tradition. 'Green Heritage' by Lefton is proof. Originally designed 25 years ago, it is the oldest Lefton line in existence and still remains one of the most popular today. In the tradition of yesteryear, highly skilled artisans hand paint each piece individually, paying the highest regard to detail and design, finishing each with pure liquid gold. 'Green Heritage' ... a collectible for generations to come. Experience the Lefton tradition."

Green Heritage has changed only slightly over the forty plus years it has been offered for sale. In determining the age of a Green Heritage item, it is helpful to know that the original pattern sold between 1962-1980 and items made between those years do not have a "0" before the item number. The 1981 Lefton catalogue had the same Green Heritage photos used in the 1980 catalogue, however the numbers for the items now had zeroes in front of the numbers to make them five digits. These same photos were used in the 1982 catalogue. New photos were used in the 1983, 1984, and 1985 catalogues that were slightly different than the previous years. These photos eliminated the "sold out" items. In 1986 a new set of photos was used; however, these photos contained the exact items that were pictured in the previous three years. This was the last year that the individually "hand painted" Green Heritage items were offered for sale.

Green Heritage – 1962
#1266. Tumble-Up. $85

Green Heritage – 1988
#05854. Cup & Saucer Dated 1984. $30

In 1987 the only Green Heritage item offered for sale was the 07543G Musical Teapot. In 1988 the new line of Green Heritage with a decal pattern was offered for sale. The numbers for these items began with 05850. What will be confusing to a collector is that you will find items pictured for the first time in the 1988 catalogue with a 1984 date on them. I believe that Lefton wanted to sell out the old line of Green Heritage before offering for sale this new line. Green Heritage items in this new line appeared in every catalogue since then until 1999, with the exception of 1998.

In the 2000 catalogue a new line of Green Heritage was introduced, and I will include it in this book because it is dated 1999. It is fitting that Lefton would introduce a new line of Green Heritage in the last year of the twentieth century. In the 1999 catalogue on the page with Green Heritage is written, "Green Heritage has been in the Lefton line for over 35 years and has withstood the test of time. Made to the same exacting standards as in 1960, it remains one of our most popular lines today." I have copies of the new Lefton Company catalogues for 2002 and 2003. Green Heritage is pictured in both those catalogs. As it says on the cover of the 2002 catalogue ... "The Legacy Lives On."

Green Heritage – 1999
#12367. 6 1/2" Pitcher. $25

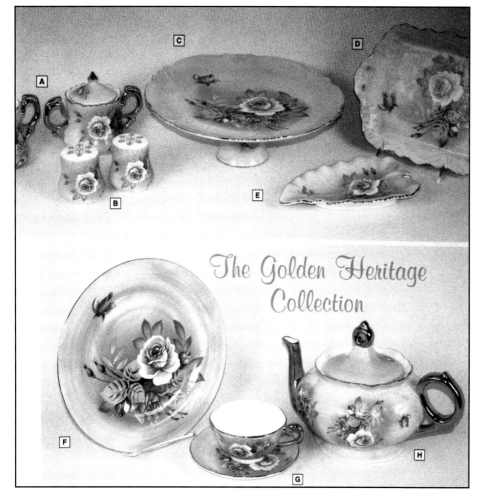

The newest Heritage pattern is "Golden Heritage." It was introduced by the new Lefton Company in 2003, and appeared for the first time in that year's catalog. It is identical to the Green Heritage line introduced in 1999, except it has a pale golden yellow background. It will be interesting to see if this pattern becomes as popular and collectible as the Brown and Green Heritage patterns. My bet is that it will!

Author's Lefton Collection

Over the years I have been asked by other Lefton collectors what items I have in my Lefton collection. Because I try to keep my collection down to a "displayable" size, I have limited my collection to items made before 1975. Most of them were made before 1965. I currently have approximately 1700 items in my collection. All the photos in my first book *Twentieth Century Lefton China and Collectibles* and all but four items in this book are of items in my personal collection.

Because no Lefton catalogue is known to exist before 1953, and because of the date corrections to the Lefton hallmarks and labels, I wanted to include photos of some items in my collection made before 1956 when the "Reg. U.S. Pat. Off." hallmarks started appearing on items. To help you date the following Lefton items, I have broken them into groups having the same hallmark or label on them.

Snack Set w/ Fruit. $55

Pink Thistle Hallmark
1946-1952

Snack Set w/ Fruit. $55

Floral Cup & Saucer w/ Gold. $65

6 3/4" Floral Square Plate. $45

5 1/2" Floral Reticulated Square Bowl. $65

Samurai Hallmark
1946-1952

Demitasse Cup & Saucer
w/ Roses. $35

Demitasse Cup & Saucer
w/ Pansies. $35

Demitasse Cup & Saucer w/ Violets. $35

Demitasse Cup & Saucer w/ French Rose. $35

"American Beauty"
Cup & Saucer. $45

"American Beauty"
Cup & Saucer. $45

"American Beauty"
Cup & Saucer. $45

Cup & Saucer, Fruit
Pattern w/ Gold. $65

Gold Cup & Saucer (Found w/
Pink Thistle Hallmark Also). $65

#494. Cup & Saucer, Pattern Similar
to 1ˢᵗ Dinnerware Pattern. $55

Cup & Saucer, Pattern Similar to 1st Dinnerware Pattern. $55

Gold Cup & Saucer, Pattern Similar to 1st Dinnerware Pattern. $60

#673. Cup & Saucer.
$48

#673. Cup & Saucer.
$48

#673. Cup & Saucer.
$48

#719. Cup & Saucer. $48

#719. Cup & Saucer. $48

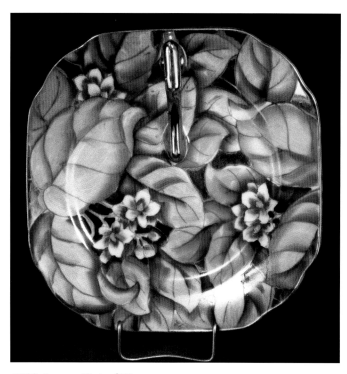

#732. Lemon Plate. $50

#767. 5" Leaf Shape Plate w/ Pansies. $45

#767. 5" Leaf Shape Plate w/ Roses. $45

Wall Plate, Hand Painted Fruit. $55

Hand Painted Lefton
Made In Occupied Japan
1946-1952

Demitasse Cup &
Saucer w/ Roses.
$35

Demitasse Cup &
Saucer w/ Roses.
$35

Demitasse Floral Cup & Saucer w/ Ribbon. $45

Demitasse Pink Orchid Cup & Saucer. $35

Lefton's Japan
1952-1954

Floral Cup & Saucer. $55

Duck Ashtray. $30

Swan Candy Dish
(Bisque). $50

LAMORE CHINA
ENTIRELY HAND
MADE
G.Z.L. USA
MADE IN
OCCUPIED JAPAN

Lamore China Entirely Hand
Made G.Z.L. U.S.A. Made in
Occupied Japan
1946-1952

Floral Cup & Saucer. $55

Lefton China Made In Japan
1952-1954

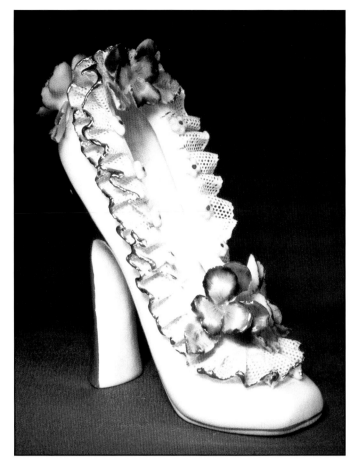

#461. 4 3/4" Lace Shoe, Pansy or Rose Trim. $55

Swan Ashtray.
$28

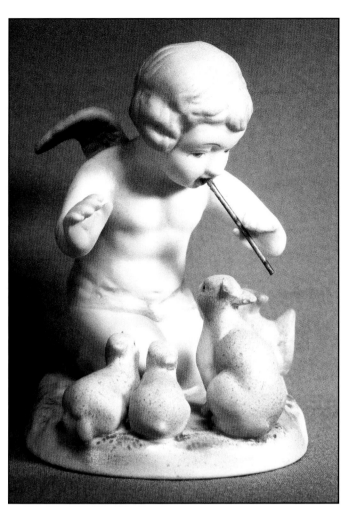

#544. 4 1/2" Angel
w/ Animals. $50

#681. Leaf Shaped Dish w/ Violets. $25

Lefton China Hand Painted
Made In Japan
1952-1954

#722. Swan
Candy Dish. $65

#813. Pitcher Vase w/ Hand Painted Roses, Pair. $75

#875. 9 1/4" Bowl in Pastel Green bisque w/ Pink Roses. $240

#780. Demitasse Cup & Saucer. $35

#966. Bisque Baby on Lace Pillow, 5 in Set. $65

#966. Bisque Baby on
Lace Pillow, 5 in Set. $65

Lefton China Hand Painted
Japan
1952-1954

#265. Three Piece Perfume Set w/ Applied Flowers. $95

#955. 5" Lyre Vases, Pair. $140

Lefton China Hand Painted (Large Crown)
1954

#195. Swan Dish w/
Applied Violets. $40

#780. Four Seasons
Plate, Spring. $40

#780. Four Seasons Cup & Saucer, Autumn. $45

#711. Reticulated Cup & Saucer. $40

#711. Reticulated
Plate. $40

#123. Perfume Bottle
(missing stopper), 3
Pieces in Set. $95

Lefton China Hand Painted
(Small Crown)
1954-1956

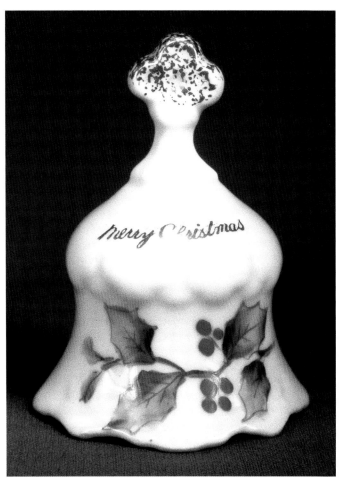

2 1/2" Bell "Merry Christmas." $35

Miniature Hands w/ Rose. $35

#989. Bisque Baby,
3 kinds. $55

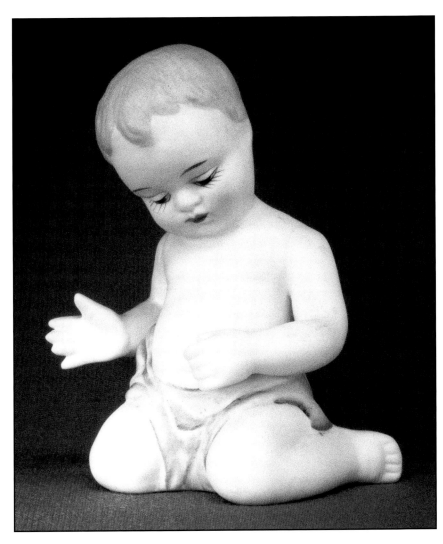

#989. Bisque Baby,
3 kinds. $55

#773. 9 1/4" Bowl in Pastel Green Bisque w/ Pink Roses. $240

#1187. Ethnic Doll w/
Real Lace "Carmen." $85

#1188. Ethnic Doll w/
Real Lace "Fifi." $85

#1189. Ethnic Doll w/ Real Lace "Maria." $85

#1190. Ethnic Doll w/ Real Lace "Zsa Zsa." $85

#8948. Girl w/
Matching Doll. $95

#8948. Girl w/ Matching Doll. $95

#8948. Girl w/
Matching Doll. $95

#052. Tumbler,
Rose or Violet. $32

#929. Hand Holding
Urn. $75

#2115. 4"
Compote. $35

#262. Ashtray w/ Applied
Bird & Roses. $32

#7060. 7" Vase w/
Applied Flowers. $65

#260. 6" Vase,
3 shapes. $55

#260. 6" Vase,
3 shapes. $55

#7086. 4" Miniature Vase, 6 shapes. $35

#7086. 4" Miniature Vase, 6 shapes. $35

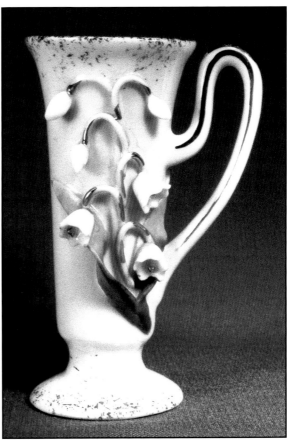

#198. 3 1/4" Miniature Vase. $35

#198. 3 1/4" Miniature Vase. $35

#7075. 6 1/2" Vase,
3 shapes. $65

#7075. 6 1/2"
Vase, 3 shapes. $65

#235. Candleholders w/ Applied Flowers. $65

#228. Kewpie Baby, 3 poses. $45

#229. Kewpie on Scroll, 3 kinds. $50

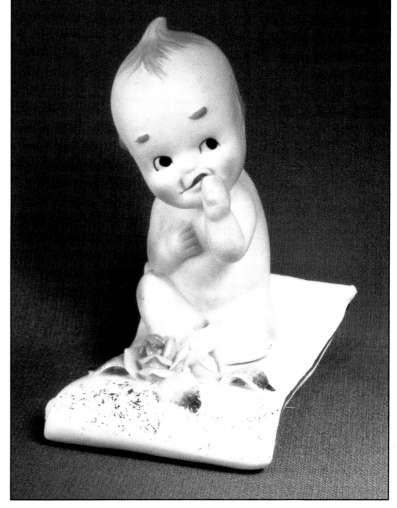

#808. 4" Angel "Going to Market," 6 kinds. $45

#808. 4" Angel "Betty Co-Ed," 6 kinds. $45

#8281. 4" Angel of the Week, 7 kinds. $45

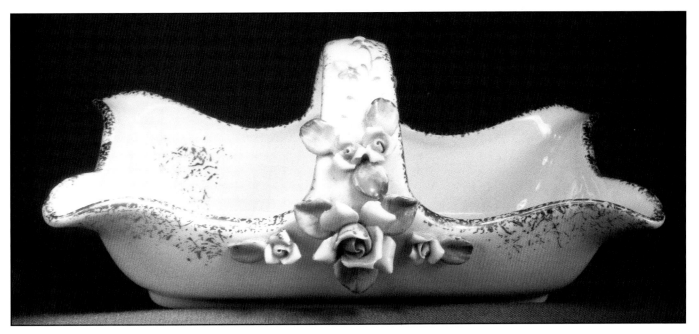

#2085. 6" Candy Basket. $65

#165. Compote. $55

#4044. 6" Bone Dish,
Elegant Rose. $30

#2048. 3 1/2" Egg Cup,
Elegant Rose. $32

Cup & Saucer,
Elegant Rose. $45

Cup & Saucer,
Elegant Violet. $45

Plate, Elegant Rose. $45

Plate, Elegant Violet.
$45

#2300. Fluted Cup & Saucer, Elegant Rose. $50

#2300. Fluted Cup & Saucer, Elegant Violet. $50

#2300. 7 1/4" Plate, Elegant Rose. $45

#2300. 7 1/4" Plate, Elegant Violet. $45

#975. Fluted Cup & Saucer, Fruit. $50

#975. 7 1/4" Plate to Match
975 Cup & Saucer. $45

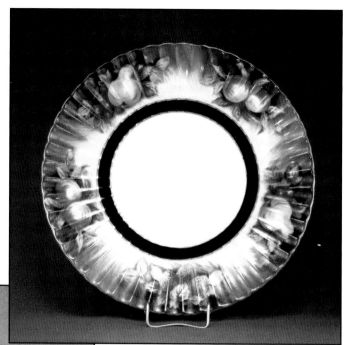

#2110. Footed AD Cup &
Saucer w/ Fruit Design. $35

#2110. Footed AD Cup &
Saucer w/ Floral Design. $35

#2173. Oriental Design Cup & Saucer (One of Lefton's Finest C&S). $55

#922. Cup & Saucer w/ Curved Rim. $40

#395. Stackable Sugar & Creamer. $48

#068. 8" Lattice Plates in
Fruit or Floral, 3 of each. $28

#4953. 5 3/4" Cigarette Box,
Dated 1955. $38

#4863. 6" Cigarette Box, Dated 1955. $38

#3053. 2 3/4" Pineapple
Shaker, Pair. $40

Lefton's Exclusives Label Found on Early
Lefton Bird Figurines

#135A. 5" Birds in Lifelike
Designs, Goldfinch. $45

#135A. 5" Birds in Lifelike
Designs, Cardinal. $45

#135A. 5" Birds in Lifelike
Designs, Oriole. $45

#135A. 5" Birds in Lifelike
Designs, Woodpecker. $45

#135A. 5" Birds in Lifelike Designs, Tanager. $45

#135B. 5" Blue Jay, 2 designs. $45

#135B. 5" Blue Jay, 2 designs. $45

#135B. 5" Cardinal, 2 designs. $45

#135B. 5" Cardinal,
2 designs. $45

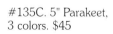

#135C. 5" Parakeet,
3 colors. $45

#135C. 5" Parakeet,
3 colors. $45

#135C. 5" Parakeet,
3 colors. $45

#8787. 5" Bird Musician,
12 kinds. $55

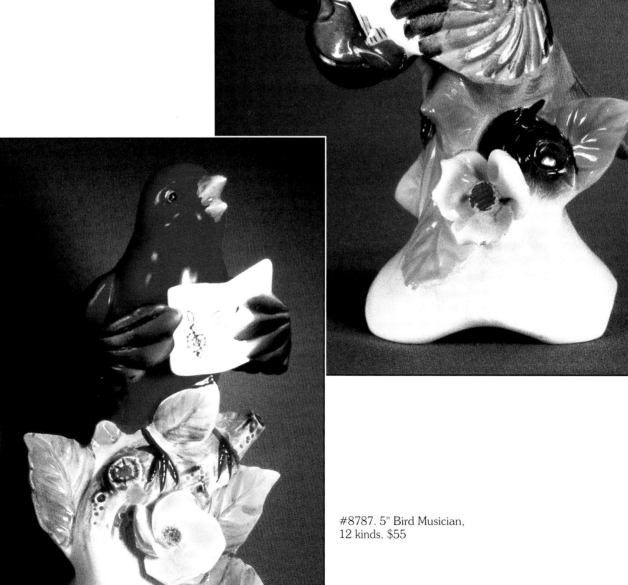

#8787. 5" Bird Musician,
12 kinds. $55

#8029. 7" Double Parakeet
Figurines, 3 colors. $70

#8029. 7" Double Parakeet
Figurine, 3 colors. $70

#8867. 5" Double Parakeet
Figurine, 3 colors. $55

#8008. 6" Cardinal, Mother
w/ Baby on Branch, 6 kinds.
$70

#8008. 6" Robin, Mother
w/ Baby on Branch, 6
kinds. $70

#8008. 6" Blue Jay, Mother w/ Baby on Branch, 6 kinds. $70

#8008. 6" Tanager, Mother w/ Baby on Branch, 6 kinds. $70

#120. 3 Baby Birds on 9"
Branch, 3 kinds. $75

#9302. 7 1/2" Fighting
Rooster, Pair. $95

Lefton's First Dinnerware Pattern

Very little is known about the early years of Lefton. The earliest known Lefton catalogue is from 1952 or 1953, so no catalogue available for research contains dinnerware made much earlier than that time frame. A clue as to what might be the first dinnerware pattern sold was found on the last page of Lefton's 1987 catalogue. It pictured a cup and saucer in a fruit pattern. The information printed under the picture states this cup is Item No. NE0010 and that there were eighty-four sets of this cup & saucer produced in 1946. (The original price was $2.00 a set). Further research uncovered an article in the July 6, 1983, issue of *Antique Trader Weekly*. The article shows a photograph of the same cup and saucer pictured in the 1987 Lefton catalogue, and describes it as being the first dinnerware pattern Lefton ever sold. Being a collector of Lefton "Made In Occupied Japan" items, I was thrilled to learn this, as I have several pieces in this pattern in my Lefton collection. Here are pictures of items made in this pattern.

Article in July 6, 1983, issue of *Antique Trader Weekly*.

Samurai Hallmark
G.Z.L.

Wall Hanging Plate. $50

Dinner Plate. $55

Cup & Saucer w/ Gold. $65

Sugar & Creamer. $45

Reticulated Square Bowl. $65

Reticulated Round
Bowl. $65

Bowl in Wood Frame.
$45

Lefton Patterns and Their Name

Here are pictures of the patterns that you will find in the price guide section of this book. When I spoke with John Lefton in April 2003, I asked him about the Lefton patterns, and who designed them. His answer was "we all did." When I questioned him further on this, he said that when someone saw a greeting card, wallpaper design, or material, etc. that they liked, they brought it in as a sample for a possible Lefton pattern. John told me that all of the Lefton items from 1960 on were designed and developed by Lefton. (Marika Berman designed some specialty lines beginning in 1953.) Lefton gave names to most of these patterns, however some were never given a name by Lefton. Over the years, collectors named these patterns. Collectors have also over the years added to, or changed some of the names that were originally Lefton's. If Lefton named a pattern, that is the name you will find in this price guide for that pattern. If it is known by another name, that name will be in parentheses next to the Lefton name. If a pattern was not named by Lefton, I have put "collector's name" in parentheses after the name. There are a few Lefton named patterns whose items in those patterns had a paper label put on them with a name different than the Lefton name. I have noted the paper label name in parentheses next to the Lefton name.

This price guide consists of Lefton's dinnerware patterns only. I have excluded the kitchenware patterns, which consist mainly of cookie jars, canister sets, spoon rests, etc. I have also eliminated any dinnerware patterns that did not consist of at least five items. This eliminated a lot of tea sets, and cups & saucers that can be found in many patterns not shown in this book.

The Lefton description for the item most recognized as a "coffee pot" is sometimes referred to in the earlier catalogues as another (larger) "teapot." To make it easier for collectors to know which item number refers to the coffee pot, I have used "coffee pot" for the larger of the two pots.

You will notice that the patterns from the 1950s and '60s had cigarette items that matched the dinnerware. Smoking at dinner was more in vogue than it is today, so cigarette holders and individual ashtrays were often placed on the table for the convenience of guests who smoked. You will find fewer cigarette items to match dinnerware introduced in the 1970s and in later years.

The date after each pattern name is the year that an item in that pattern first appeared in a Lefton catalogue. This pattern may have been introduced with only a couple of items in that pattern, and additional pieces added in later years if the original pieces were popular sellers. Items in each pattern were offered for sale for approximately three to seven years after it was introduced, which will help in dating your dinnerware items. There are of course some exceptions, such as items in the popular "Green Holly/Hollyberry" and the "Heritage" patterns. It would have taken more time than I was willing to spend to keep track of what years each item in this price guide was offered for sale. Green Heritage is the number one selling dinnerware pattern, and it is the longest selling dinnerware pattern, so I did take the time to keep track of what years every piece in the Green Heritage pattern was offered for sale. You will see that information in parentheses after each item in that pattern.

I have noticed that several items have a date on them that match the year they first appeared in a Lefton catalogue, while others have a date on them that is a year (or more) earlier than when they first appeared in a Lefton catalogue. I can't explain these differences, however for consistency, the date next to the pattern name in the price guide section of this book is the year that pattern was first seen in a Lefton catalogue, and first offered for sale. Keep in mind that an item might in fact have been made a year or more before the year it first appeared in a Lefton catalogue. The most accurate date will be the one on the item.

It is hard to tell the exact date of any pre-1953 dinnerware items except by hallmark, as no Lefton catalogue before 1953 was available for research. I have been able to date the earliest Elegant Rose and Elegant Violet items to 1952 because the stacking sugar & creamer #958, and the stacking teapot, creamer & sugar #985 are featured in a Lefton ad placed in the January 1953 issue of *Gift & Art Buyer's* magazine. These items would have had to be made in 1952 to be in the January 1953 magazine.

Americana
#939. 9 1/4" Plate w/ Handle. $50

Barnyard Melodies (Fruit or Rooster)
#2590. 7" Vinegar Bottle. $28.
#2593. 6" 16 Oz. Pitcher. $55
Compliments of Stuart Brown

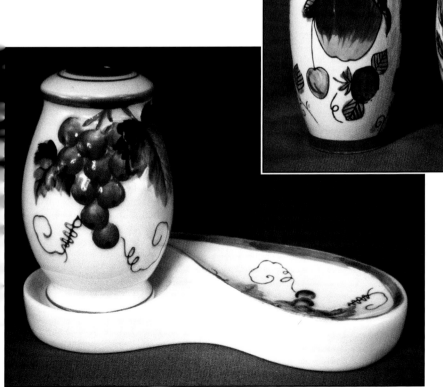

Berry Harvest
#313. Spoon Rest w/ Salt
Shaker. $45

Blue Heaven
#3037. Coffee Pot. $55

Blue Paisley
#2334. Jam Jar w/ Plate & Spoon. $45

Bluebird
#282. Salt & Pepper Shakers. $50

Bossie The Cow
#6512. 4 1/2" Sugar & Creamer. $45

Boughs of Holly
#03031. 3 3/4" Footed Mug. $10

Brown Heritage Floral
#468. 7 1/2" Candy Box. $150

Canton Rose
#04498. 5" Bell. $10

Brown Heritage Fruit
#20131. Tidbit Tray. $35

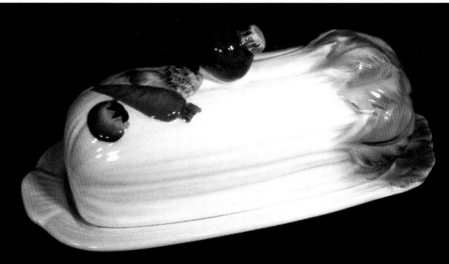

Celery Line
#1301. Butter Dish. $30

Christmas Cardinal
#1206. 4" Napkin Holder. $15

Christmas Holly
#7950. Cup & Saucer. $28

Christmas Hollyberries
#10409. 7" Dish. $14

Christmas Ribbon
Items for sale in 1988

Christmas Rose
#07679. 5 1/2" Oval Dish.
$17

Christmas Tree
#3339. 10" Two Compartment Dish. $65

Christmas Tree w/ Presents
#1064. 8" Plate. $20

Cissy Cabbage (Cabbage Cutie)
#2127. Sugar & Creamer. $75

Cosmos
#1083. Compote. $48

Cotillion (Blue)
#3195. 7 1/2" Plate. $55

Cotillion (Pink)
#3187. Sugar & Creamer. $65

Country Charm (Blue or Gold)
#4614. Jam Jar w/ Spoon. $30

Country Garden
#5934. Jam Jar w/ Spoon. $15

Country Squire
#1608. Salt & Pepper Shakers. $25
Courtesy of Stuart Brown

Crimson Rose
#674. 7 1/2" Plate. $28

Cuddles
#1449. Sugar & Creamer. $45

Dainty Miss
#322. Sugar & Creamer. $80

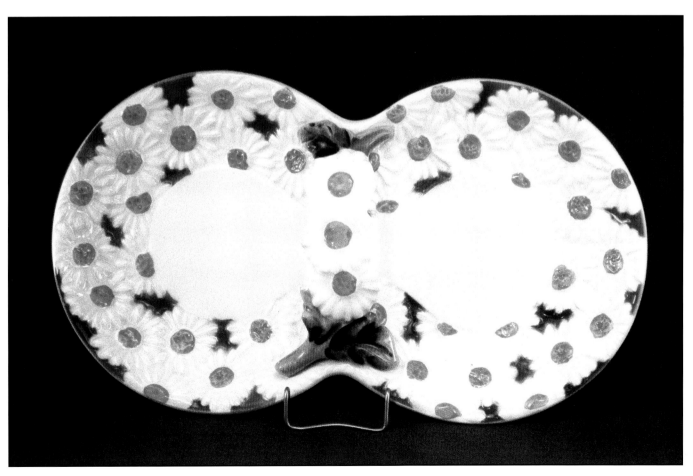

Daisytime
#492 Two Compartment Dish. $36.00

Dancing Leaves
#7278. 8 1/2" Compote. $28

Della Robbia
#1742. Cookie Jar. $70

Dimity Rose
#6319. Sugar & Creamer. $55

Dutch Blue
#3921. Instant Coffee Jar w/ Spoon. $30

Dutch Girl
#2366. Cookie Jar. $175

Early American Rooster
#1020. Candy Box. $48

Elegant Rose
#885. Stacking Teapot, Creamer, Sugar. $90

Elf Head
#3970. Sugar & Creamer (not shown). $95

Elegant Violet
#985. Stacking Teapot, Creamer, Sugar. $90

Espresso
#3159. Wisteria Coffee Pot, Cream & Sugar. $90

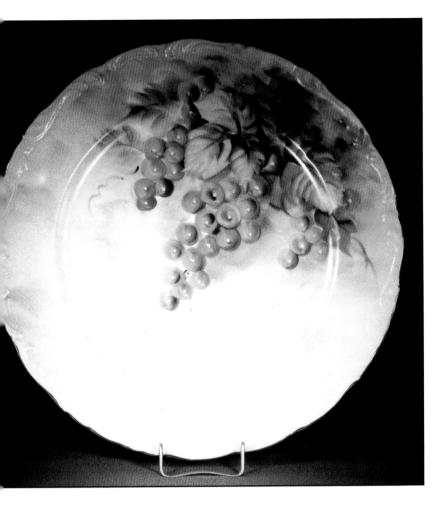

Fiesta (w/Fruit)
#5349. 5" Mug. $15

Festival
#2621. 9" Plate. $28

Fleur De Lis
#3004. 2 3/4" Sugar & Creamer. $16
Courtesy of Stuart Brown

Floral Bouquet
#7157. 5 3/4" Jam Jar. $22

Floral Chintz
#8034. Sugar & Creamer. $56

Forget-Me-Not (Blue Floral)
#4177. Cup & Saucer. $25

French Rose
#4063. 2 Cup Teapot. $35

Fruit Basket (Tutti Fruit Label)
#1670. Large Pitcher. $60

Fruit Delight
#3113. 5" Jam Jar. $20

Fruit Fantasia
#6727. 5 1/2" Jam Jar. $24

Fruits of Italy
#1209. 3 1/2" Mug. $13

Garden Bouquet
#3476. Sugar & Creamer. $65
Courtesy of Stuart Brown

Garden Bouquet
#08282. 5" Teabag Holder. $12

Garden Daisy
#1561 4 1/2" Cache Pot. $18

Gingham
#3307. Covered Butter Dish. $26
Courtesy of Stuart Brown

Golden Flower
#239. 6 Cup Teapot. $45

Golden Laurel
#2442. Two Tier Tidbit Tray. $65

Golden Leaf
Items for sale in 1965.

Golden Rose
#1406. 6 Cup Teapot. $45

Golden Tree
#1872. Three Compartment Dish. $75

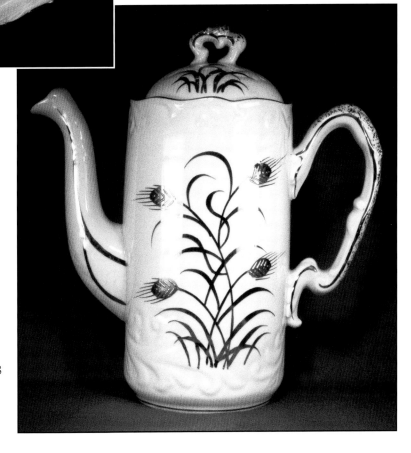

Golden Wheat
#2568. Coffee Pot. $68

Grape Line
#2663. Teapot. $90

Green Heritage (Early)
#510. Tall Teapot. $165

Green Heritage
#796. 6 1/2" Pitcher. $95

Green Holly/Hollyberry
#161. 6" Plate. $18

Green Orchard (Green Pear N Apple)
#3761. Canister, Four in Complete Set. $125

Green Vintage (Green Heritage Fruit)
#6278. 4 1/2" Candy Box. $65

Heavenly Rose
#2758. Cup & Saucer. $40

Heirloom (Heirloom Elegance)
#5393. 4 1/2" Candy Box. $75

Heirloom Rose
#1915. Condiment Set. $74

Holiday Garland
Items for sale in 1977.

Heirloom Violet
#1074. Snack Set. $48

Holly Garland
#1964. Coffee Pot. $125

Holly Leaves and Berries
#05245. 9" Two Tier Tidbit Tray. $48

Honey Bee (Bee Line Label)
#1285. Cheese Dish w/ Cover. $45

Holly w/ Touches of Candy Cane Red
#1294. 8" Tree Shaped Nappy Dish. $36

Hot Poppy
#4597. 4" Basket. $15

Lilac Chintz
#693. Teapot. $175

Masonic
#4345. Ashtray. $8.00

Magnolia
#2518. Coffee Pot. $87

Midnight Rose
#07391. 3" Box. $10

Miss Priss
#1503. 4" Mug. $75

Misty Rose
#5696. 5" Compote. $40

Moss Rose
#3171. Snack Set. $26

Mr. Toodles
#3293. Childs Bowl & Mug. $95

Mushroom Forest
#6465. 7" Gravy Boat. $26

Order of Eastern Star
#3788. Salt & Pepper Shakers. $10

Paisley Fantasia
#6796. 5" Sugar & Creamer. $40

Pear N Apple (Mustard)
#4130. Cookie Jar. $68

Pear and Apple (White)
#4262. Bone Dish. $18

Petites Fleurs
#6433. Bathroom Dish, Set. $38

Pinecone
#350. 5 1/4" Candleholder, Pair. $40

Pink Clover
#2507. 9 1/4" Plate. $28

Pink Daisy
#5161. Chip n Dip Plate. $75

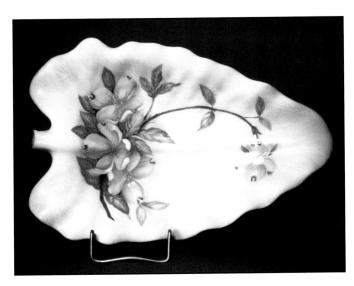

Pink Dogwood
07254. Leaf Shaped Bon-Bon Dish,
3 kinds. $18

Poinsettia
#06433. Cup & Saucer. $30

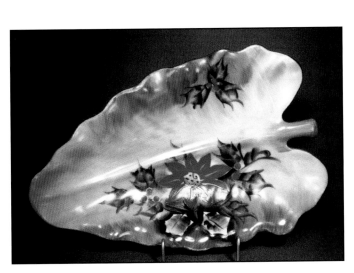

Poinsettia (Limited Edition)
#4394. 7" Nappy Dish. $25

Rose Chintz
#3185. 2 Cup Teapot. $55.

Rose Garden/Tan
#6956. 9 1/2" Silent Butler. $115

Rose Chintz (w/ Purple Flowers)
#7245. Miniature Sugar Bowl, Set. $18

Rose Garden/Green
#6957. 9 1/2" Silent butler. $115

Rose Garden/White
#6712. 2 Cup Teapot. $55

Rustic Daisy
#3855. Teapot. $55

Shamrock Porcelain
#03083. Cup & Saucer. $23

Silver Wheat
#225. Sugar & Creamer. $25

Simplicity
Items for sale in 1961.

Spring Bouquet
#4585. 5 1/2" Pitcher w/ Bowl. $60

Spring Bouquet (Butterflies)
#688. 2" AD Cup & Saucer. $23

Sweet Violets
#2880. 8" Two Compartment Dish.
$32

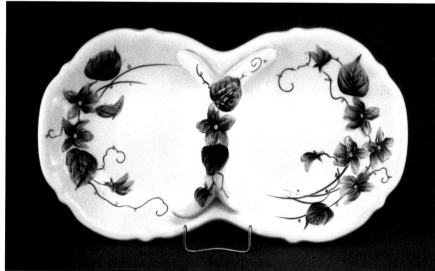

Symphony in Fruit
#1018. Two Compartment Dish. $23

Thumbelina (Honey Bun)
#1697. Jam Jar. $65

Tisket A Tasket
#7297. 7 3/4" Covered Butter Dish. $28

To A Wild Rose
#2581. 7 1/2" Candy Box. $85

Vineyard
#3029. Sugar & Creamer. $38

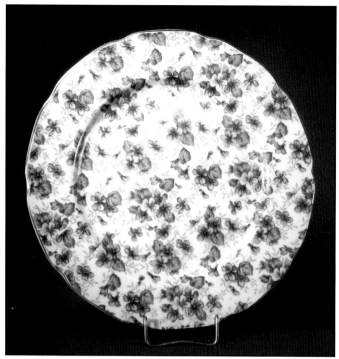

Violet Chintz (Chintz Violet)
#658. 7 1/2" Plate. $28

Wheat Poppy
#1228. Cookie Jar. $40

White Christmas
#604. Sugar & Creamer. $40

White Classic
#7016. Soup Tureen
w/ Tray & Ladle. $100

Yellow Tulip
#7127. 7 1/2" Covered Butter Dish. $45

White Holly
#6054. 7 1/2" Cookie Jar. $75

Yuletide Holly
#7802. Coffee Pot. $60

Bibliography

Books

Barton, Karen. *Twentieth Century Lefton China and Collectibles.* Atglen, Pennsylvania: Schiffer Publishing, Ltd., 2001.

Advertisements, Articles, and Catalogues

Geo. Zoltan Lefton Company. *Yearly and specialty/holiday catalogues issued to retail dealers for the purpose of buying and selling new items in Gift Stores from the following years:* 1953, 1954, 1955, 1956, 1957 Specialty Catalogue, 1958, 1959, 1959 Specialty Catalogue, 1960, 1961, 1962, 1963, 1963 Specialty Catalogue, 1964, 1964 Specialty Catalogue (Fall and Christmas Supplement), 1965, 1965 Specialty Catalogue, 1966 (Supplement to 1965 Catalogue), 1967-68, 1967 Specialty Flyer, 1968-69, 1968 Specialty Flyer, 1968 Specialty Selections, 1969, 1969 Fall Flyer, 1970, 1970 Specialty Catalogue/Gifts of Quality by Lefton, 1971, 1971-72 Specialty Flyer for All Occasions, 1972-73, 1972-1973 Specialty Catalogue, 1973, 1973-74 Specialty Catalogue/Holiday Book, 1974, 1975, 1975-76 Specialty Catalogue/Holiday Book, 1976, 1976-77 Specialty Catalogue/Holiday Book, 1977, 1977 Specialty Catalogue/Holiday Book, 1978, 1978-79 Specialty Catalogue/Holiday Book, 1979, 1980, 1980 Specialty Catalogue/Holiday Book, 1981, 1981 Specialty Catalogue/Holiday Book, 1981 Specialty Catalogue/Christmas Book, 1981 Lefton China, An Introductory Guide to Collecting, 1982, 1982 Specialty Catalogue/Holiday Book, 1982 Specialty Catalogue/Christmas Book, 1983 Specialty Catalogue/Holiday Book, 1983 Specialty Catalogue/Christmas Catalog, 1984, 1984 Specialty Catalogue/Holiday Book, 1984 Specialty Catalogue/Christmas Collection, 1985, 1985 Specialty Catalogue/Holiday Book, 1985 Specialty Catalogue/Christmas Collection, 1986, 1986 Specialty Catalogue/Holiday Collection, 1986 Specialty Catalogue/Christmas Book, 1987, 1987 Specialty Catalogue/Christmas, 1988, 1988 Specialty Catalogue/Holiday Collection, 1988 Specialty Catalogue/Christmas, 1989, 1989 Specialty Catalogue/Holiday Collection, 1990, 1990 Specialty Catalogue/Holiday Collection, 1991, 1991 Specialty Catalogue/50 years of Celebrating the Holidays, 1992, 1992 Specialty Catalogue/Christmas, 1993, 1993 Specialty Catalogue/Holiday Gift Collection, (no 1994 Yearly Catalogue was published), 1994-95 Specialty Catalogue/Holiday Book, 1995, 1995 Specialty Catalogue/Holiday Book, 1996, 1996 Specialty Catalogue/Christmas Book, 1997, 1997 Specialty Catalogue/Christmas, 1998, 1999, 1999 Specialty Catalogue/Holiday, 2000, 2001, 2002, 2003.

Lefton Ads in *Gift and Art Buyer* magazine for the following issues: May 1946, May 1952, January 1953, April 1953, July 1953, September 1953, August 1954, January 1955, August 1955, September 1955.

Lefton Ads in *Giftwares* magazine for the following issues: January 1953, February 1953, June 1953, July 1953, September 1953, February 1954, March 1954, June 1954, September 1954, October 1954.

Lefton Article in July 6, 1983 issue of *Antique Trader Weekly.*

Twentieth Century Lefton Dinnerware and Accessories Price Guide

AMERICANA – 1959

		*O.P.	C.B.V.
160	12" Celery Dish	$1.00	$65
162	9" Wooden Salad Fork & Spoon	$0.50	$30
164	10" Bowl	$1.75	$70
937	9" Three Compartment Dish	$1.50	$65
938	9 3/4" Two Compartment Dish	$1.00	$55
939	9 1/4" Plate w/ Handle	$0.80	$50
940	8" Compote	$1.25	$65
942	Two Tier Tidbit Tray	$1.80	$75
943	7 1/4" Cookie Jar	$2.00	$90
944	5" Candy Box	$1.00	$60
945	4 3/4" Spice Set	$2.50	$60
946	4 Piece Canister Set	$4.50	$125
947	6 1/4" Candle Holder, Pair	$1.25	$35
948	9 1/4" Bowl	$1.50	$70
949	4 1/4" Candle Holder	$1.00	$35
950	8 1/4" Oil & Vinegar Bottles	$1.50	$80
951	6 1/2" Wall Pocket	$1.00	$40
952	Tea Pot	$1.50	$115
953	Sugar & Creamer	$1.00	$50
955	Salt & Pepper	$0.55	$25
956	Jam Jar w/ Spoon & Under Plate	$0.80	$45
957	Snack Set	$0.80	$35
958	Butter Dish	$0.75	$65
959	4 1/2" Pitcher	$0.80	$55
960	Egg Cup	$0.30	$35
961	Spoon Rest w/ Salt Shaker	$0.60	$65
962	8 1/4" Gravy Boat	$1.25	$65
963	16 Piece Starter Set	$6.00	$450
965	14" Platter	$1.80	$75
966	7 1/4" Soup Bowl	$0.55	$40
967	8 1/4" Bowl	$1.00	$45
968	Match Box	$0.75	$45
969	Salt Box	$1.00	$45
970	6" Bowl	$0.50	$35
971	11" Dish	$1.25	$65
972	15 1/4" Dish	$2.00	$85
973	Cup & Saucer	$0.55	$30
974	6 3/4" Plate	$0.35	$21
976	10 1/2" Plate	$0.90	$45
977	9 1/4" Plate	$0.60	$35
978	9 1/2" Covered Vegetable Bowl	$2.00	$95
979	9 1/4" Bowl	$1.38	$85
980	12 1/4" Cake Plate w/ Cutter	$2.50	$95
1243	7" x 11" Bowl	$1.50	$55
1244	12" Platter	$1.25	$65
1587	4 3/4" Jam Dish w/ Spoon	$1.00	$45
1980	7 1/2" Plate	$0.50	$25

2015	6" Pitcher	$1.25	$45
3237	6" Tile	$0.40	$30
3243	2 Cup Teapot	$0.80	$55
3317	10 3/4" Compote	$1.75	$55

*O.P. = Original Price
C.B.V. = Current Book Value

BARNYARD MELODIES – 1955

		O.P.	C.B.V.
2580	7" Combination Teapot/Sugar/ Creamer, also in Fruit design	$1.10	$110
2581	Cup & Saucer, also in Fruit design	$0.35	$35
2582	9" Plate, also in Fruit Design	$0.40	$40
2583	8 Cup Teapot, also in Fruit Design	$1.50	$150
2584	4 Cup Teapot, also in Fruit Design	$0.55	$55
2585	Sugar & Creamer, also in Fruit Design		$0.55 $55
2586	4 1/2" Jam Jar on tray w/cover & spoon, also in Fruit Design	$0.55	$55
2587	3 1/2" Egg Cup, also in Fruit Design	$0.30	$30
2588	3 1/2" Salt & Pepper, also in Fruit Design	$0.30	$30
2589	7" Covered Butter Dish, also in Fruit Design	$0.50	$50
2590	7" Oil & Vinegar Bottles, also in Fruit Design	$0.55	$55
2591	11" Two Compartment Dish, also in Fruit Design	$0.80	$80
2592	5" 8 oz. Pitcher, also in Fruit Design	$0.33	$33
2593	6" 16 oz. Pitcher, also in Fruit Design	$0.55	$55
2594	7 1/2" 24 oz. Pitcher, also in Fruit Design	$0.90	$90
2595	4" Salt & Pepper w/ Handle, also in Fruit Design	$0.50	$50

BERRY HARVEST – 1958

		O.P.	C.B.V.
291	9" Three Compartment Dish	$1.50	$65
292	9 3/4" Two Compartment Dish	$1.00	$55
293	Handled Relish Dish	$1.25	$65
294	7 1/4" Cookie Jar	$2.00	$90
296	8" Compote	$1.25	$65
297	5" Candy Box	$1.00	$60
298	Sugar & Creamer	$1.00	$50
299	Jam Jar w/ Plate & Spoon	$0.80	$45
300	6 1/4" Candle Holder, Pair	$1.25	$35
301	Salt & Pepper Shakers	$0.55	$25
302	Cup & Saucer	$0.55	$30
303	10 1/2" Plate	$0.90	$45

No.	Item	O.P.	C.B.V.
304	6 3/4" Plate	$0.35	$21
305	8" Plate	$0.60	$35
306	6" Bowl	$0.50	$35
308	14" Platter	$1.80	$75
309	12 1/4" Cake Plate	$1.80	$75
310	Egg Cup	$0.30	$35
311	Butter Dish	$0.75	$65
312	4 1/2" Pitcher	$0.80	$55
313	Spoon Rest w/ Salt Shaker	$0.60	$65
314	4 Piece Canister Set	$4.50	$125
315	Spice Set	$2.50	$60
316	Oil & Vinegar Bottles	$1.50	$80
317	Two-Tier Tidbit Tray	$1.80	$75
318	Salt Box	$1.00	$45
319	Match Box	$0.75	$45
430	Teapot	$1.50	$115
431	9 1/4" Plate w/ Handle	$0.80	$50
434	Pitcher & Bowl Wall Pocket	$1.00	$40
572	Snack Set	$0.80	$35
629	Cup & Saucer	$0.55	$30
669	16 Piece Starter Set	$5.50	$175
861	6" Trivet	$0.55	$30
873	Cake Serving Knife	$0.30	$25

BLUE HEAVEN (BLUE ROSE) – 1962

No.	Item	O.P.	C.B.V.
3037	Coffee Pot	$1.50	$55
3038	Sugar & Creamer	$1.00	$30
3039	Jam Jar w/ Plate & Spoon	$0.80	$25
3040	Salt & Pepper Shakers	$0.40	$14
3041	Cookie Jar	$1.75	$60
3323	9 1/4" Plate	$0.65	$17

BLUE PAISLEY – 1964

No.	Item	O.P.	C.B.V.
1972	Coffee Pot	$2.25	$95
1974	Sugar & Creamer	$1.25	$45
1975	Two Tier Tidbit Tray	$2.10	$50
2131	Egg Cup	$0.40	$35
2133	Cup & Saucer	$1.10	$25
2134	AD Cup & Saucer	$0.65	$25
2141	6" Dish w/ Handle	$0.55	$30
2142	Candy Box	$1.60	$35
2154	Pin Boxes, 3 kinds	$0.30	$12
2159	3 1/2" Mug	$0.40	$15
2169	5 1/2" Pitcher Vase, 3 shapes	$0.60	$20
2170	6 1/4" Bud Vase, 3 shapes	$0.65	$25
2173	5 1/2" Lamps, 2 shapes	$0.55	$40
2181	7" Bowl	$0.60	$45
2185	7 3/4" Dish	$1.35	$40
2201	Three Compartment Dish	$1.35	$65
2334	Jam Jar w/ Plate & Spoon	$1.05	$45
2337	9 1/4" Plate	$0.80	$35
2338	7 1/4" Plate	$0.50	$25
2339	Cup & Saucer	$0.60	$25
2340	Snack Set	$0.65	$25
2341	Compote	$0.75	$28
2343	Nested Ashtrays	$0.75	$20
2344	5" Ashtray	$0.35	$15
2346	Salt & Pepper	$0.40	$28
2347	6" Bone Dish	$0.40	$18
2348	Single Tidbit Tray	$0.65	$20
2349	6 1/2" Dish, 2 kinds	$0.65	$20
2350	Cigarette Urn w/ 2 Trays	$0.65	$23
2351	Sugar & Creamer w/ Tray	$1.10	$45
2354	Tea Bag Holder	$0.25	$13
2357	3 1/4" Ash Tray	$0.25	$10
2358	Mini Sugar & Creamer, 2 kinds	$0.65	$37
2359	8" Bone Dish	$0.60	$18
2360	Ashtray/Cigarette Holder	$0.50	$22
2373	Teapot	$2.25	$95
2374	Sugar & Creamer	$1.10	$32
2716	4 1/2" Candy Box	$1.10	$30
2725	2 3/4" Mug	$0.33	$15
4649	17 Piece Starter Set	$6.50	$350

BLUEBIRD – 1958

No.	Item	O.P.	C.B.V.
057	Bird w/ Babies Wall Plaque, Blue, Green, Yellow	$1.00	$200
151	5 1/2" Spoon Rest w/ Salt	$1.00	$200
239	Salt & Pepper Shakers, Bluebirds w/ Stones	$1.25	$145
267	Bank, Bluebird w/ Stones	$2.25	$225
282	Salt & Pepper Shakers	$0.50	$50
283	6 1/2" Wall Pockets (Mr. & Mrs. Bluebird)	$1.75	$325
284	4" Mug	$0.50	$60
286	Egg Cup	$0.30	$70
287	4 1/2" Pitcher	$0.50	$95
288	6" Planter	$1.00	$150
289	Cookie Jar	$2.00	$350
290	Sugar & Creamer	$0.80	$95
435	Bowl	$0.90	$65
436	Jam Jar w/ Spoon	$0.90	$95
437	Cheese Dish	$1.20	$325
438	Teapot	$2.20	$325
788	Musical Teapot "Tea for Two"	$4.20	$350
3551	Salt & Pepper	$0.65	$45
3552	Baby Set, 4 1/2" Mug & 6" Bowl	$1.25	$120

BOSSIE THE COW – 1971

No.	Item	O.P.	C.B.V.
6509	4 1/2" Jam Jar w/ Spoon	$1.25	$30
6510	3 1/2" Salt & Pepper	$1.10	$25
6511	8" Spoon Rest	$1.10	$28
6512	4 1/2" Sugar & Creamer	$1.75	$45
6513	3 1/2" Mug	$0.80	$15
6514	7 3/4" Butter Dish w/ Cover	$1.75	$30
6515	6 1/2" Pitcher w/ 6 1/2" Bowl	$2.75	$55
6516	8 1/4" Pitcher	$2.10	$65

BOUGHS OF HOLLY – 1982

No.	Item	O.P.	C.B.V.
00239	9" Bell	$7.50	$20
00242	4" Basket	$2.50	$10
03026	7" Teapot	$15.00	$55
03027	Sugar & Creamer	$6.00	$25
03028	Cup & Saucer	$3.75	$18
03029	10" Plate	$5.00	$25
03030	8" Plate	$2.50	$20
03031	3 3/4" Footed Mug	$2.50	$10
03032	4" Mug	$2.25	$12
03033	3 1/4" Pitcher w/ Bowl	$3.25	$18
03034	2 1/2" Salt & Pepper	$3.00	$15
03035	5" Bell	$2.75	$10

No.	Item	O.P.	C.B.V.
03036	9" Two Tier Tidbit Tray	$11.00	$45
03043	4" Dish	$2.00	$14
03044	7 1/2" Dish	$4.50	$22
03047	2" Pin Box, 3 kinds	$1.75	$10
03048	6 1/2" Vase, 3 kinds	$3.00	$18
03049	5 3/4" Dish	$4.50	$16
03050	3 3/4" Bag	$3.25	$12
03051	6 Napkin Rings	$7.50	$28
03052	3" Candleholder	$2.50	$12
03053	4 1/2" Candleholder	$2.50	$18
03054	3 1/4" Box	$1.75	$14
03055	Napkin Holder	$2.50	$18
03057	3 1/2" Bag	$3.00	$14
03058	3 1/4" Bell	$1.75	$14
03059	3" Dish	$2.00	$15
03862	3" Basket	$2.00	$15
03867	4 3/4" Bell	$4.00	$18
03868	5" Dish	$2.50	$15
03869	5 1/2" Dish	$3.00	$18

BROWN HERITAGE FLORAL (HERITAGE, FLORAL HERITAGE) – 1956

No.	Item	O.P.	C.B.V.
048	10 3/4" Chocolate Pot	$3.00	$350
051	9" Pitcher	$2.00	$115
055	Sugar & Creamer	$1.75	$65
062	9" Coffee Pot (Rare- sold 1964-67)	$2.75	$295
068	Sugar & Creamer	$1.75	$65
072	Cup& Saucer	$1.25	$45
113	9 1/4" Plate	$1.25	$45
117	Compote	$2.00	$95
120	10" Compote	$2.00	$95
185	9" Plate w/ Plastic Handle	$0.75	$65
328	3 1/4" Pitcher & Bowl	$0.50	$40
468	7 1/2" Candy Box	$3.00	$150
476	2 Cup Teapot	$0.75	$65
481	6 1/4" Bone Dish	$0.45	$28
563	8" Bone Dish	$0.65	$44
613	2 3/4" Salt & Pepper Shakers	$0.30	$30
703	Cup & Saucer	$0.75	$37
1264	Pitcher w/ Tumbler (Tumble-Up)	$2.50	$95
1317	Two Tier Tidbit Tray	$3.00	$75
1861	9 1/2" Cake Plate	$3.50	$65
1862	5 1/2" Bud Vase	$1.50	$35
1863	7 3/4" Teapot	$2.50	$125
1864	Snack Set	$0.75	$38
1865	Cup & Saucer	$1.50	$55
1866	Coffee Pot	$2.50	$125
1867	Cream & Sugar	$1.50	$55
1868	Nappy Dish	$1.50	$40
1869	6" Bone Dish	$0.75	$30
1870	4 1/2" Candy Dish	$2.50	$85
1871	8 3/4" Vase, 3 kinds	$2.75	$85
1872	3 1/4" Pitcher & Bowl	$1.75	$35
1873	5 1/2" Pitcher & Bowl	$3.25	$65
1874	6 1/4" Pitcher & Bowl	$5.00	$85
1882	7 1/4" Plate	$0.55	$37
1883	Cup & Saucer	$0.30	$37
1990	7" Compote	$1.00	$45
2222	9" Plate	$1.00	$45
2274	Compote	$1.00	$65
2635	2 1/2" Cup & Saucer	$0.85	$38
2721	4 1/2" Candy Box	$1.75	$67

No.	Item	O.P.	C.B.V.
2761	Jam Jar w/ Plate & Spoon	$1.10	$50
2763	5 1/2" Vases, 3 kinds	$0.60	$28
3112	Teapot	$3.00	$185
3114	8 Cup Pitcher	$2.50	$110
3116	8 3/4" Vases, 3 kinds	$2.00	$65
3118	3 1/4" Vases, 3 kinds	$0.40	$28
3288	3 1/2" Pitcher & Bowl	$1.00	$45
4239	13" Oil Lamp	$4.00	$210
4277	11" Oil Lamp	$2.00	$175
7543	9 1/2" Musical Teapot "Tea For Two"	$5.50	$65
20127	Nappy Dish, 3 shapes	$0.55	$42
20128	Coasters	$0.25	$18
21029	Two Tier Tidbit Tray (1956)	$5.00	$95
20130	Snack Set (1956)	$1.50	$38
20131	Tidbit Tray (1956)	$1.50	$35
20334	4 1/2" Dishes, 3 kinds (1956)	$0.35	$30
30132	Salt & Pepper Shakers (1956)	$0.60	$35

BROWN HERITAGE – 1985

No.	Item	O.P.	C.B.V.
04149	Cup & Saucer	$7.50	$30
04150	AD Cup & Saucer	$5.50	$22
04151	4 1/2" Sugar & Creamer	$15.00	$48
04152	Teapot	$20.00	$80
04153	7 1/2" Plates	$3.75	$15
04154	Cup & Saucer	$6.00	$24
04155	5 1/2" Bud Vases, 3 kinds	$4.50	$18
04156	9 1/4" Dish	$9.00	$36
04157	Nappy Dish, 3 kinds	$4.50	$18
04158	9" Plate	$6.00	$24
04159	8 3/4" Vase, 3 kinds	$12.00	$48
04698	2 1/4" Salt & Pepper	$5.00	$20

BROWN HERITAGE FRUIT (HERITAGE) – 1956

No.	Item	O.P.	C.B.V.
072	Cup & Saucer	$1.25	$45
113	9 1/2" Plate	$1.25	$55
117	9" Compote	$2.00	$95
469	7 1/2" Candy Box	$3.00	$150
478	2 Cup Teapot	$0.75	$65
480	6 1/2" Bone Dish	$0.45	$28
561	Cup & Saucer	$1.00	$45
562	7 1/4" Plate	$0.55	$37
563	8" Bone Dish	$0.65	$44
607	Salt & Pepper Shakers	$0.30	$30
689	Compote	$2.00	$95
704	Cup & Saucer	$0.75	$37
1265	Pitcher w/ Tumbler (Tumble-Up)	$1.75	$95
1315	Two Tier Tidbit Tray	$3.00	$75
1992	Compote	$1.00	$65
2222	9" Plate	$1.00	$45
2636	2 1/2" Cup & Saucer	$0.85	$38
2720	4 1/2" Candy Box	$1.75	$67
2760	Salt & Pepper	$0.45	$28
2762	Jam Jar	$1.10	$50
2764	5 1/2" Vases, 3 kinds	$0.60	$28
3113	Teapot	$3.00	$185
3115	8 Cup Pitcher	$2.50	$110
3117	8 3/4" Vases 3 kinds	$2.00	$85
3118	3 1/4" Vases, 3 kinds	$0.40	$28
3289	3 1/2" Pitcher & Bowl	$1.00	$45
4283	11" Oil Lamp	$2.00	$210
20127	Nappy Dishes, 3 kinds (1956)	$0.55	$42

20128	3" Coaster (1956)	$0.15	$18
20129	Two Tier Tidbit Tray (1956)	$5.00	$95
20130	Snack Set (1956)	$0.75	$38
20131	Single Tidbit Tray (1956)	$1.50	$35
20334	4 1/2" Nappy Dishes (1956) 3 kinds	$0.35	$30
20591	9" Coffee Pot (1957)	$2.50	$155
20592	4 1/2" Sugar & Creamer (1957)	$1.50	$75
30132	Salt & Pepper Shakers (1956)	$0.60	$35

CANTON ROSE – 1982

		O.P.	C.B.V.
00226	10" Plate	$10.00	$25
00232	8" Plate	$4.50	$14
00233	8" Temple Jar	$12.00	$30
00234	8" Ginger Jar	$12.00	$30
00235	7" Planter w/ Tray	$10.00	$25
00236	7 1/2" Bowl	$10.00	$25
00237	10 3/4" Compote	$15.00	$38
03374	10 1/2" Two Tier Tidbit Tray	$15.00	$38
03375	10" Vase	$13.50	$34
03376	6" Teapot	$12.50	$32
03377	4 1/2" Sugar & Creamer	$10.00	$25
03725	4 3/4" Frame	$4.00	$10
03726	7" Frame	$9.00	$22
03727	7" Double Frame	$9.00	$22
04495	7" Frame	$9.00	$22
04496	4 3/4" Frame	$3.75	$10
04497	7" Double Picture Frame	$9.00	$22
04498	5" Bell	$3.00	$10
04499	6" Vase	$4.00	$11
05000	3 1/2" Mug	$2.50	$10

CELERY LINE – 1960

		O.P.	C.B.V.
327	11 3/4" Celery Tray	$1.00	$40
1295	13" Egg Plate	$1.50	$60
1296	Tea Pot	$1.50	$60
1297	Sugar & Creamer	$1.00	$40
1298	Jam Jar	$0.80	$32
1299	Spoon Rest w/ Salt Shaker	$0.60	$24
1300	Cheese Dish	$1.00	$40
1301	Butter Dish	$0.75	$30
1302	9 1/2" Two Compartment Dish	$1.00	$40
1303	9" Bowl w/ Fork & Spoon	$2.00	$80
1304	7 1/2" Cookie Jar	$1.50	$60
1305	5 1/2" Pitcher	$0.80	$32
1306	Oil & Vinegar Bottles	$1.50	$60
1307	Salt & Pepper	$0.60	$24
1308	10 3/4" Three Compartment Dish	$1.25	$50

CHRISTMAS CARDINAL – 1977

		O.P.	C.B.V.
1061	8" Plate	$1.65	$20
1062	4" Mug	$1.25	$12
1063	3 3/4" Footed Mug	$1.35	$10
1067	2 1/2" Salt & Pepper	$1.65	$15
1068	3 1/4" Pitcher w/ Bowl	$2.10	$18
1069	5" Bell	$1.75	$12
1070	6 1/4" Vase, 3 kinds	$1.65	$18
1071	10 1/4" Cake Plate w/ Handle	$4.00	$32
1072	10 1/4" Cake Plate	$7.00	$48
1203	3 1/4" Pin Box	$1.10	$14
1205	3 1/2" Bell	$0.90	$12

1206	4" Napkin Holder	$1.75	$15
1207	6" Nappy Dish, 3 kinds	$2.25	$18
1252	8" Compote	$4.00	$32
1260	8 1/2" Coffee Pot	$7.00	$48
1261	Sugar & Creamer	$5.50	$30
1297	Cup & Saucer	$2.25	$18
1655	8" Teapot	$8.75	$55
1656	3 1/2" Cream & Sugar	$6.00	$35
1657	10 1/4" Plate	$4.00	$32
1762	AD Cup & Saucer	$1.50	$15
2055	3 3/4" Planter	$2.25	$18
2096	5" Dish	$3.00	$20
2104	6" Dish	$3.00	$20
2109	9 1/4" Cake Plate	$5.00	$35
2154	1" Thimble (Gift Boxed)	$1.40	$10
8269	9" Two Tier Tidbit Tray	$8.00	$48

CHRISTMAS CARDINAL – 1981

		O.P.	C.B.V.
00244	4" Basket	$2.50	$10
01061	8" Plate	$2.50	$20
01062	4" Mug	$2.25	$12
01063	3 3/4" Footed Mug	$1.90	$10
01067	2 1/2" Salt & Pepper	$3.00	$15
01068	3 1/4" Pitcher w/ Bowl	$3.25	$18
01069	5" Bell	$2.75	$10
01070	6 1/4" Vase, 3 kinds	$3.00	$18
01071	10 1/4" Cake Plate w/ Handle	$7.00	$32
01203	3 1/4" Pin Box	$1.75	$14
01205	3 1/2" Bell	$1.75	$14
01206	4" Napkin Holder	$2.50	$18
01207	6" Nappy Dish, 3 kinds	$3.00	$16
01297	Cup & Saucer	$3.75	$18
01655	8" Teapot	$12.00	$55
01656	3 1/2" Cream & Sugar	$6.00	$35
01657	10 1/4" Plate	$5.00	$32
01760	8" Dish	$5.00	$22
02055	3 3/4" Bag Planter	$3.25	$14
02104	6" Dish	$3.00	$16
02154	1" Thimble (Gift Boxed)	$2.00	$10
02279	4" Dish	$1.75	$14
02450	5 3/4" Dish	$2.50	$16
02511	5" Candy Box	$5.50	$33
02525	4" Planter	$3.25	$18
02653	9" Bell	$7.50	$20
RE2829	5" Jewel Box	$7.50	$20
02845	3 1/2" Candleholder	$2.50	$12
02848	4 1/2" Bell	$4.00	$18
02851	6 1/2"Vase	$4.00	$18
02966	5" Dish	$2.50	$15
03041	6 Napkin Rings, Set	$7.50	$28
03042	3" Basket	$2.00	$15
03628	7 1/2" Dish	$4.25	$22
04532	10" Plate	$5.00	$25
04533	8" Plate	$2.60	$20
04534	3 3/4" Footed Mug	$2.50	$10
04535	4" Mug	$2.50	$12
04536	Cup & Saucer	$4.00	$18
04537	7" Teapot	$12.00	$55
04538	Sugar & Creamer	$7.50	$35
04539	9" Two Tier Tidbit Tray	$12.00	$48
04540	7 1/2" Tree Shaped Dish	$4.25	$20
04541	5 3/4" Leaf Dish	$2.50	$15

04542	5 1/2" Oval Dish	$3.25	$20
04543	5" Round Dish	$2.50	$15
04544	6 1/2" Bud Vase, 3 kinds	$3.00	$18
04545	4 1/2" Pitcher w/ Bowl	$3.50	$20
04546	Salt & Pepper	$3.00	$15
04547	5" Bell	$3.00	$18
04550	3" Pin Box	$1.75	$14
04551	4" Card Holder	$2.50	$18
04552	3 1/2" Bell	$2.75	$14
04553	3 1/2" Candleholder	$3.00	$12
04554	4 1/2" Candleholder	$3.50	$18
04555	3" Basket	$2.00	$10
04556	2" Pin Box, 3 kinds	$2.00	$10
04613	4 1/4" Hurricane Lamp w/ Candle	$4.00	$18
04697	AD Cup & Saucer	$3.00	$18
04719	6 Napkin Rings	$7.50	$28
04829	3 1/2" Bag Planter	$3.00	$14
05015	5 1/2" Dish	$3.00	$18
05848	3 1/2" Mug	$3.25	$12
05973	7 1/4" Bud Vase, 3 kinds	$3.00	$22
05975	2 1/4" Pin Box	$2.00	$10
05977	4" Basket	$3.00	$15
05979	4 3/4" Basket	$3.00	$15
06645	6 1/2" Leaf Shape Dish	$5.50	$22
06646	6 1/2" Flower Shape Dish	$5.50	$22
06647	6 1/2" Teardrop Shape Dish	$5.50	$22
06806	3 3/4" Footed Mug	$3.25	$10
08269	9" Two Tier Tidbit Tray	$10.00	$48

CHRISTMAS CARDINAL – 1994

		O.P.	C.B.V.
01207	10" Plate w/ Server	$20.00	$40
01212	3 3/4" Napkin Holder	$6.00	$12
01213	6" Bell Shape Dish	$6.00	$12
01233	10 1/4" Plate	$10.00	$20
01234	9" Plate	$9.00	$18
01235	8" Plate	$9.50	$19
01236	7" Plate	$7.00	$14
01237	6" Vase	$7.00	$14
01238	7 1/2" Tree Shape Dish	$9.00	$18
01239	6" Leaf Shape Dish	$5.50	$11
01240	6 1/2" Oval Dish	$7.00	$14
01241	5" Round Dish	$6.00	$12
01242	9" Tray	$15.00	$30
01243	5" Bell	$6.50	$13
01244	2 1/2" Salt & Pepper	$6.50	$13
01245	4" Mug	$5.00	$10
01246	7" Teapot	$20.00	$40
01247	Sugar & Creamer	$14.00	$28
01248	Cup & Saucer	$8.50	$17
01249	3 3/4" Candleholder	$7.00	$14

CHRISTMAS HOLLY – 1973

		O.P.	C.B.V.
001	3 3/4" Footed Mug	$1.25	$10
453	3 1/4" Pin Box	$0.90	$14
457	3 1/4" Bell	$0.70	$14
569	3" Planter	$1.00	$15
1764	AD Cup & Saucer	$1.50	$18
2056	3 3/4" Planter	$3.00	$14
2097	5" Dish	$3.00	$15
2103	6" Dish	$3.00	$16
7940	3 1/4" Pitcher & Bowl	$1.75	$15

7941	5 3/4" Pitcher & Bowl	$3.75	$18
7942	6 1/4" Bud Vase, 3 kinds	$1.10	$18
7943	4 1/2" Candy Box	$2.25	$15
7944	5 1/4" Bell	$1.10	$10
7945	4 1/2" Candleholder, Pair	$2.25	$18
7946	6 3/4" Nappy Dish	$1.35	$16
7947	5 1/2" Jam Jar w/ Spoon	$1.75	$30
7948	8" Teapot	$6.50	$55
7949	4 1/2" Sugar & Creamer	$2.75	$35
7950	Cup & Saucer	$1.35	$28
7951	AD Cup & Saucer	$1.00	$16
7952	7 1/4" Plate	$1.10	$20
7953	9" Plate	$1.50	$25
7954	9" Two Tier Tidbit Tray	$5.00	$45
7955	2 1/2" Salt & Pepper	$1.00	$15
7956	7" Compote	$1.75	$15
8190	8" Tree Dish	$2.75	$22
8191	8" Bell Dish	$2.75	$20
8192	9 1/4" Compartment Dish	$3.75	$22
8193	7" Ashtray	$1.50	$10
8194	4" Planter	$2.75	$14

CHRISTMAS HOLLY – 1981

		O.P.	C.B.V.
00001	3 3/4" Footed Mug	$2.50	$10
00453	3 1/4" Pin Box	$1.75	$14
00457	3 1/4" Bell	$1.75	$14
02056	3 3/4" Planter	$3.25	$12
02280	4" Dish	$1.75	$14
02451	5 3/4" Dish	$2.50	$16
02526	4" Planter	$3.25	$18
02654	9" Bell	$7.50	$20
RE2828	5" Jewel Box	$7.50	$35
02844	3 1/2" Candleholder	$2.50	$12
02847	4 1/2" Bell	$4.00	$18
02850	6 1/2" Vase	$4.00	$18
02967	5" Dish	$2.50	$15
04830	3 1/2" Bag Planter	$3.00	$14
04839	7 1/2" Dish	$4.25	$22
04843	3" Basket	$1.75	$15
07940	3 1/4" Pitcher & Bowl	$3.25	$18
07942	6 1/4" Bud Vase, 3 kinds	$3.00	$18
07944	5 1/4" Bell	$2.75	$10
07945	4 1/2" Candleholder, Pair	$3.50	$18
07948	8" Teapot	$12.00	$55
07949	4 1/2" Sugar & Creamer	$6.00	$35
07950	Cup & Saucer	$3.75	$18
07952	7 1/4" Plate	$2.50	$20
07953	9" Plate	$3.50	$25
07954	9" Two Tier Tidbit Tray	$10.00	$45
07955	2 1/2" Salt & Pepper	$3.00	$15
08306	2-4" Pin Boxes, 4 kinds	$3.00	$10

CHRISTMAS HOLLYBERRIES – 1996

		O.P.	C.B.V.
10404	10" Cake Plate w/ Server	$20.00	$40
10405	4" Napkin Holder	$5.50	$11
10406	6" Bell Shape Dish	$6.00	$12
10407	10 1/4" Plate	$10.00	$20
10408	8" Plate	$7.50	$15
10409	7" Dish	$7.00	$14
10410	6 1/2" Oval Dish	$7.00	$14
10411	7 1/2" Tree Shape Dish	$8.50	$17

10412	6 1/2" Tree Shape Dish	$7.00	$14
10413	6" Leaf Dish	$5.00	$10
10414	5" Round Dish	$5.00	$10
10415	9" Tray	$15.00	$30
10416	5" Bell	$6.00	$12
10417	2 1/2" Salt & Pepper	$6.00	$12
10418	4" Mug	$5.00	$10
10419	7" Teapot	$20.00	$55
10420	Sugar & Creamer	$13.00	$35
10421	Cup & Saucer	$8.50	$17
10422	3 3/4" Candleholder	$6.50	$13

CHRISTMAS RIBBON – 1988

		O.P.	C.B.V.
06445	10" Plate	$6.50	$25
06446	8" Plate	$3.75	$20
06447	Cup & Saucer	$6.00	$18
06448	3 1/4" Mug	$3.25	$10
06449	3 3/4" Salt & Pepper	$4.00	$15
06450	2 1/8" Pin Box	$2.75	$10
06451	3 1/2" Candleholder	$3.50	$12
06452	5" Bell	$3.75	$10
06453	6" Vase	$3.50	$18
06454	5" Box	$5.00	$20
06455	3 1/2" Bell	$2.50	$14

CHRISTMAS ROSE – 1991

		O.P.	C.B.V.
07666	7 1/2" Teapot	$20.00	$55
07667	Sugar & Creamer	$15.00	$35
07674	3 3/4" Covered Box	$6.50	$14
07675	4 3/4" Covered Box	$10.00	$28
07676	3 1/2" Candleholder	$7.50	$15
07678	6" Vase	$7.00	$18
07668	Cup & Saucer	$8.00	$18
07669	Salt & Pepper	$6.00	$15
07670	10" Plate	$12.00	$25
07671	8" Plate	$7.50	$20
07672	6" Plate	$4.00	$13
07673	3 3/4" Footed Mug	$5.50	$12
07679	5 1/2" Oval Dish	$8.00	$17

CHRISTMAS TREE – 1963

		O.P.	C.B.V.
2687	8 1/4" Plate	$0.55	$30
2834	4 1/8" Mug	$0.45	$22
2885	Cup & Saucer	$0.65	$35
2886	9 1/4" Plate	$0.65	$35
2887	Sugar & Creamer	$1.25	$60
2888	Teapot	$1.75	$90
3320	8 1/4" Single Tidbit Tray	$0.75	$40
3339	10" Two Compartment Dish	$1.10	$65
3340	Tree Shaped Salt & Pepper	$0.60	$35
3341	3" Mug	$0.30	$20
3348	Candy Box	$0.75	$45
3351	9 1/4" Two Tier Tidbit Tray	$2.00	$98
3364	8" Tree Shaped Bonbon	$0.80	$50

CHRISTMAS TREE (w/ Presents) – 1977

		O.P.	C.B.V.
1064	8" Plate	$1.65	$20
1065	4" Mug	$1.25	$12
1066	3 3/4" Footed Mug	$1.35	$15

1073	10 1/4" Footed Cake Plate	$7.00	$35
1074	3 1/2" Pitcher w/ Bowl	$2.10	$18
1075	2 1/2" Salt & Pepper	$1.65	$15
1198	3 1/4" Covered Box	$1.10	$14
1199	3 1/2" Bell	$0.90	$14
1200	8 1/4" Dish	$3.75	$25
1201	8 1/2" Dish	$3.75	$25
1202	4" Napkin Holder	$1.75	$18
1253	8" Compote	$4.00	$32
1263	8 1/2" Coffee Pot	$7.00	$50
1264	Sugar & Creamer	$5.50	$35
1295	10 1/4" Cake Plate w/ Metal Handle	$4.00	$32
1298	2 1/2" Cup & Saucer	$2.25	$18
1658	8" Teapot	$8.75	$55
1659	3 1/2" Sugar & Creamer	$6.00	$35
1650	10 1/4" Plate	$4.00	$25
1763	AD Cup & Saucer	$1.50	$18
2054	6" Dish, 2 kinds	$2.75	$18
2098	5" Dish	$3.00	$18
2105	6" Dish	$3.00	$18
3106	12 1/2" Platter	$8.50	$50
2107	9 1/4" Plate	$5.00	$25
8268	6 1/4" Vase, 3 kinds	$2.00	$18
8270	9" Two Tier Tidbit Tray	$8.00	$48

CISSY CABBAGE (CABBAGE CUTIE) – 1964

		O.P.	C.B.V.
2123	Teapot	$1.75	$95
2125	Spoon Rest	$0.50	$50
2126	Salt & Pepper Shakers	$0.60	$45
2127	Sugar & Creamer	$1.25	$75
2128	Jam Jar w/ Plate & Spoon	$1.00	$60
2129	8" Dish	$1.00	$65
2130	Cookie Jar	$2.00	$115

COSMOS (Collector's Name) – 1959

		O.P.	C.B.V.
1077	Teapot	$2.00	$120
1078	Sugar & Creamer	$1.00	$50
1079	Cup & Saucer	$0.55	$38
1080	7 1/2" Plate	$0.50	$35
1081	9" Plate	$0.60	$42
1082	Snack Set	$0.65	$42
1083	Compote	$0.70	$48
1084	5" Candy Box	$0.65	$45
1085	6" Lemon Plate	$0.45	$32

COTILLIAN, BLUE (Collector's Name) – 1962

		O.P.	C.B.V.
3191	Coffee Pot	$1.50	$95
3192	Sugar & Creamer	$1.00	$65
3193	Cup & Saucer	$0.60	$35
3194	2 1/2" Cup & Saucer	$0.50	$30
3195	7 1/2" Plate	$0.50	$55

COTILLIAN, PINK (Collector's Name) – 1962

		O.P.	C.B.V.
3186	Coffee Pot	$1.50	$95
3187	Sugar & Creamer	$1.00	$65
3188	Cup & Saucer	$0.60	$35
3189	2 1/2" Cup & Saucer	$0.50	$30
3190	7 1/2" Plate	$0.50	$55

COUNTRY CHARM – 1967
Blue

		O.P.	C.B.V.
4611	Cookie Jar	$2.50	$75
4612	Canister Set	$6.50	$150
4613	2 3/4" Mug	$0.50	$20
4614	Jam Jar w/ Spoon	$0.80	$30
4615	6" Instant Coffee w/ Spoon	$0.80	$35
4616	6 1/2" Salt & Pepper	$1.00	$40
4617	7 1/2" Double Spoon Rest	$0.55	$35
4618	Teapot	$2.00	$85
4619	Sugar & Creamer	$1.25	$50

Gold

		O.P.	C.B.V.
4602	Cookie Jar	$2.50	$75
4603	Canister Set	$6.50	$150
4604	2 3/4" Mug	$0.50	$20
4605	Jam Jar w/ Spoon	$0.80	$30
4606	6" Instant Coffee w/ Spoon	$0.80	$35
4607	6 1/2" Salt & Pepper	$1.00	$40
4608	7 1/2" Double Spoon Rest	$0.55	$35
4609	Teapot	$2.00	$85
4610	Cream & Sugar	$1.25	$50

COUNTRY GARDEN – 1969

		O.P.	C.B.V.
5929	Cookie Jar	$3.50	$35
5930	Canister Set	$8.50	$85
5931	12 1/2" Square Five Compartment Dish	$3.00	$30
5932	12" Round Three Compartment Dish	$3.00	$30
5933	6 3/4" Pitcher	$2.00	$20
5934	Jam Jar w/ Spoon	$1.10	$15
6132	5 1/2" Pitcher w/ 6 1/2" Bowl	$2.00	$20
6133	8" Square Ashtray	$1.10	$11
6177	18 1/2" Platter	$5.00	$50
6178	12" Egg Plate w/ Salt & Pepper	$2.25	$25
6179	11" Relish Dish	$1.25	$13
6192	7" Candy Box	$2.50	$25
6195	6 1/2" Teapot	$2.75	$45
6196	4" Sugar & Creamer	$1.75	$30
6197	Cup & Saucer	$1.50	$15
6198	7 1/2" Plate	$1.50	$18
6199	9" Plate	$1.75	$20
6223	3 Quart Soup Tureen	$13.50	$135
6225	6" Salt & Pepper	$1.75	$18
6241	6 1/2" Cart Planter	$1.75	$18
6242	7 1/2" Covered Butter Dish	$1.50	$25
6243	5 1/2" Napkin Holder	$1.50	$15
6244	Two Tier Tidbit Tray	$3.50	$38
6300	4" Mug	$0.80	$8
6301	7 1/2" Double Spoon Rest	$0.75	$15

COUNTRY SQUIRE – 1960

		O.P.	C.B.V.
1589	6 1/2" Plate	$0.35	$30
1594	10" Two Compartment Dish	$1.00	$50
1595	10 3/4" Chip & Dip	$2.00	$100
1596	10" Three Compartment Dish	$1.50	$75
1597	Butter Dish	$0.80	$40
1598	11" Cake Set w/ Cutter	$2.00	$100
1599	3 3/4" Tea Bag Holder	$0.30	$23
1600	Four Piece Canister Set	$4.80	$195

1601	12 1/2" Egg Tray	$1.50	$75
1602	12" Cheese Tray	$1.10	$55
1603	9" Spoon Rest	$0.60	$40
1605	Single Tidbit Tray	$2.00	$100
1606	6 Cup Teapot	$1.50	$85
1607	Sugar & Creamer	$1.00	$50
1608	Salt & Pepper	$0.55	$25
1609	7 1/4" Cookie Jar	$2.00	$100
1610	4 1/2" Jam Jar w/ Spoon	$1.00	$50
1611	7" Hors d'oeuvre Holder	$1.00	$50
1612	7 3/4" Wall Pocket	$0.75	$40
1613	5 1/2" Candle Holder, Pair	$1.25	$55
1614	9" Plate w/ Handle	$0.80	$40
1615	Candy Box	$1.25	$60
1967	Cup & Saucer	$0.55	$30
1968	Mug	$0.50	$25
1969	14" Platter	$1.80	$90
1970	Egg Cup	$0.30	$25
1971	10" Salad Bowl	$1.75	$85
1972	6" Bowl	$0.50	$25
1973	6 1/2" Plaque	$0.35	$20
1974	9 1/4" Plate	$0.60	$30
1975	12" Celery Dish	$0.90	$45
1976	7" Pitcher	$1.50	$75
2239	16 Piece Starter Set	$6.00	$300
2393	5 1/4" Butter Dish w/ Lid	$1.00	$50
2648	10 1/2" Plate	$0.90	$45

CRIMSON ROSE (Collector's Name) – 1958

		O.P.	C.B.V.
096	Compote	$0.55	$35
197	Single Switch Cover	$0.25	$18
200	Double Switch Cover	$0.40	$25
250	Jumbo Cup & Saucer	$0.40	$25
566	11 Piece Breakfast Set	$3.50	$125
672	Two Tier Tidbit Tray	$2.00	$62
673	Cup & Saucer	$0.50	$31
674	7 1/2" Plate	$0.45	$28
675	9" Plate	$0.60	$37
1476	Tea Bag Holder	$0.30	$20
4995	4 Nesting Ashtrays	$0.55	$30

CUDDLES (Collector's Name) – 1978

		O.P.	C.B.V.
1446	9 1/2" Cookie Jar	$11.00	$125
1448	8" Coffee Pot	$5.50	$95
1449	4" Sugar & Creamer	$5.50	$45
1450	5 1/4" Salt & Pepper	$2.75	$25
1451	4 1/4" Jam Jar	$2.75	$45
1452	5" Napkin Holder	$2.50	$35

DAINTY MISS – 1956

		O.P.	C.B.V.
040	7 1/2" Cookie Jar	$2.00	$250
321	Tea Pot	$1.50	$170
322	Sugar & Creamer	$1.10	$80
323	Jam Jar w/ Spoon	$0.80	$80
325	Spoon Rest w/ Shaker	$1.30	$125
439	Salt & Pepper	$0.50	$50
648	Tea Bag Holder	$0.30	$35
936	Cup & Saucer	$0.80	$75
1276	9 1/2" Three Compartment Dish	$1.50	$150
1277	10" Two Compartment Dish	$1.00	$125

5707	7 3/4" Planter (1957)	$0.75	$135
6767	5" Wall Pockets, Left & Right (1956)	$1.50	$160
7797	5" Head Vase (1957)	$1.00	$110
50264	7 1/2" Girl Wall Pocket, Pair (1957)	$3.00	$225
50275	5" Girl Head Wall Pocket, Pair (1957)	$1.50	$200

DAISYTIME – 1963

		O.P.	C.B.V.
490	9" Three Compartment Dish	$2.00	$65
492	10 1/4" Two Compartment Dish	$1.25	$36
493	9 1/2" Plate	$0.80	$28
495	4 1/4" Flower Pot	$0.50	$15
496	Cup & Saucer	$0.65	$22
497	7 1/2" Plate	$0.60	$20
521	3 1/2" Egg Cup	$0.30	$15
522	3 1/2" Mug	$0.40	$14
523	2 Cup Teapot	$0.85	$40
3358	Jam Jar w/ Plate & Spoon	$0.90	$30
3359	Sugar & Creamer	$1.25	$35
3360	Teapot	$2.00	$65
3361	Cookie Jar	$2.10	$80
3362	3 3/4" Salt & Pepper	$0.65	$22
3363	Covered Butter Dish	$1.00	$32
3406	5 1/2" Pitcher	$1.10	$35
3407	6 1/4" Cheese Dish	$1.10	$35

DANCING LEAVES – 1972

		O.P.	C.B.V.
7275	12 1/2" Oval Tray	$3.25	$32
7276	9 3/4" Cookie Jar	$5.00	$50
7277	Canister Set	$15.00	$110
7278	8 1/2" Compote	$2.50	$28
7279	14" Compartment Dish	$4.00	$40
7280	5 1/4" Pitcher w/ 6" Bowl	$2.50	$25
7281	12" Egg Plate w/ Salt & Pepper	$3.25	$32
7282	3 Quart Soup Tureen w/ Tray & Ladle	$15.00	$125
7283	6" Salt & Pepper	$1.75	$17
7284	5" Jam Jar w/ Spoon	$1.50	$15
7285	Teapot	$3.25	$45
7286	Sugar & Creamer	$2.25	$25
7308	5 1/2" Napkin Holder	$2.00	$20
7309	Covered Butter Dish	$2.25	$25
7310	7" Double Spoon Rest	$1.00	$10

DELLA ROBBIA – 1964

		O.P.	C.B.V.
1742	Cookie Jar	$2.00	$70
1744	18 1/2" x 14 1/2" Platter	$2.50	$87
1950	Compote	$1.50	$50
1958	Jam Jar w/ Spoon	$0.65	$28
1961	13" Five Compartment Dish	$2.00	$70
1962	13" Three Compartment Dish	$2.00	$70
2089	7" Candy Box	$1.65	$52
2090	10" x 8" Relish Dish	$0.80	$28
2091	13" x 7" Two Compartment Dish	$1.25	$38
2092	11" x 6" Relish Dish	$0.80	$28
2485	13" Cake Plate	$3.00	$105
3486	9 3/4" Fruit Pyramid	$2.00	$70
3487	Canister Set	$5.40	$125
4135	Sugar & Creamer	$1.25	$38
4136	Teapot	$2.00	$70
4160	12 1/2" Lavabo Set	$2.00	$70

4233	Salt & Pepper	$0.65	$23
4234	Cup & Saucer	$0.65	$23
4235	7" Plate	$0.75	$28
4236	9" Plate	$1.10	$38
4917	12" Egg Plate w/ Salt & Pepper	$2.00	$70
5230	12" Chip & Dip	$3.25	$110
5231	5" Pitcher w/ 6" Bowl	$1.50	$52
5232	2 Quart Tureen w/ Ladle & Tray	$7.50	$150

DIMITY ROSE – 1971

		O.P.	C.B.V.
6315	Tea Pot	$4.50	$95
6316	8" Tall Coffee Pot	$4.50	$95
6317	7 1/4" Tumble-Up	$3.25	$70
6318	4 1/2" Jam Jar w/ Plate & Spoon	$2.00	$45
6319	Sugar & Creamer	$2.75	$55
6320	10 1/2" Cake Plate w/ Metal Handle	$1.75	$36
6321	5 1/2" Bud Vase, 3 Shapes	$0.80	$18
6322	8" Tea & Toast	$1.75	$36
6323	4 Nested Ashtrays	$1.25	$25
6324	Cup & Saucer	$1.10	$28
6325	6" Candy Box	$3.50	$70
6326	6" Pitcher w/ 9 1/2" Bowl	$4.50	$95
6327	5 1/4" Pitcher w/ 7" Bowl	$2.75	$55
6328	3 1/2" Pitcher w/ 4 1/2" Bowl	$1.50	$32
6329	9" Plate	$1.50	$32
6330	7 1/2" Plate	$1.10	$25
6331	2 1/2" Salt & Pepper	$0.90	$20
6332	6 1/4" Bone Dish	$0.75	$15
6333	Nappy Dish, 3 shapes	$1.10	$23
6334	6 1/4" Bud Vase, 3 shapes	$0.80	$18
6335	8 1/4" Vase, 3 shapes	$2.50	$52
6410	2 Piece Bathroom Set	$1.75	$36
7543	9 1/4" Musical Teapot "Tea For Two"	$5.50	$75

DUTCH BLUE – 1966

		O.P.	C.B.V.
3616	6 Piece Spice Set w/ Wood Rack	$2.50	$112
3666	Canister Set	$6.00	$185
3667	Jam Jar w/ Spoon	$0.60	$27
3668	4" Mug	$0.30	$13
3669	Cookie Jar	$2.75	$120
3670	Teapot	$1.25	$65
3671	Sugar & Creamer	$0.80	$36
3919	7 1/2" Double Spoon Rest	$0.35	$23
3920	10" Lavabo Set	$1.50	$70
3921	Instant Coffee Jar w/ Spoon	$0.65	$30
3922	4 1/2" Garlic Crusher	$1.00	$45
3923	3 1/2" Egg Cup	$0.35	$19
3924	7 3/4" Covered Cheese Dish	$1.35	$60
3925	Covered Butter Dish	$0.75	$45
3926	Salt & Pepper Shakers	$0.60	$27
3927	Egg Tray Set, 3 Pieces	$1.50	$67

DUTCH GIRL – 1961

		O.P.	C.B.V.
2366	Cookie Jar	$2.50	$175
2367	Salt & Pepper	$0.60	$42
2697	Jam Jar w/ Spoon	$0.65	$45
2698	Sugar & Creamer	$1.10	$75
2699	Teapot	$1.50	$200
3318	Planter	$0.80	$50

EARLY AMERICAN ROOSTER – 1963

		O.P.	C.B.V.
001	5" Spoon Rest or Ashtray	$0.60	$33
743	12" Rooster	$3.00	$96
1019	Cookie Jar	$2.50	$80
1020	Candy Box	$1.50	$48
1021	Jam Jar w/ Plate & Spoon	$1.00	$32
1022	Sugar & Creamer	$1.00	$32
1023	Salt & Pepper	$0.60	$20
1024	9" Roosters, Pair	$3.00	$96
1319	Spoon Rest or Ashtray	$0.55	$20
1329	9 1/4" Teabag Holder	$0.30	$15
2099	10" Bread Tray	$2.00	$64
2100	Teapot	$2.50	$80
2101	9" Tidbit Tray	$1.50	$48
2102	Match Box	$1.00	$32
2103	Salt Box	$1.25	$40
2104	10" Double Dish	$1.50	$48
2105	Canister Set	$6.00	$175

ELEGANT ROSE (Collector's Name) – 1952

		O.P.	C.B.V.
088	5 Piece Smoking Set	$2.00	$125
134	Cup & Saucer	$0.50	$32
134	7 1/2" Plate to match Cup & Saucer	$0.45	$30
134	9" Plate to Match Cup & Saucer	$0.60	$38
395	Stackable Sugar & Creamer	$0.55	$35
634	Cup & Saucer	$1.00	$40
676	Salt & Pepper	$0.50	$20
678	Cream & Sugar	$0.55	$22
700	Teapot w/ Twist Ribbing	$3.00	$120
702	Cream & Sugar w/ Twist Ribbing	$1.10	$44
885	Stacking Teapot Creamer & Sugar	$2.25	$90
928	5" Dish	$0.45	$18
929	5" Hand Holding Vase	$1.50	$60
934	Stacking Leaf Ashtrays, 3 in Set	$1.10	$44
938	Compote w/ Hand Held Base	$1.75	$70
958	Stacking Cream & Sugar	$1.50	$30
974	5" English Colonial Style Sugar & Creamer	$1.10	$44
985	Stacking Teapot, Cream & Sugar	$2.25	$90
1806	Jumbo Cup & Saucer	$1.25	$50
2032	7 1/2" Teapot	$2.50	$100
2048	Egg Cup	$0.50	$20
2124	8" Shell Shaped Snack Set	$1.10	$44
2125	Three Legged Cup & Saucer	$0.60	$32
2275	Ribbed Teapot	$1.50	$95
2276	Ribbed Cream & Sugar	$1.00	$40
2300	Ribbed Cup & Saucer	$1.00	$40
2300	Matching Ribbed Plate	$1.00	$40
2323	4 Cup Teapot w/ Swirl Pattern	$2.75	$110
2326	Sugar & Creamer	$1.10	$44
2327	6 1/2" Stacking Tea Set	$1.50	$60
2328	Tea Cup & Saucer	$1.00	$40
2330	Compote	$1.00	$40
2333	Two Tier Tidbit Tray	$1.50	$60
2351	6" Three Section Tidbit Plate	$1.10	$44
2393	Stacking Sugar & Creamer	$1.10	$44
2505	Sugar & Creamer	$1.00	$40
2562	9" Covered Candy Jar	$3.50	$140
2564	Stacking Sugar & Creamer	$1.50	$60
2565	4" Pitchers, 4 kinds	$1.10	$44
2643	AD Tall Cup and Saucer	$1.20	$50

		O.P.	C.B.V.
2736	Cup & Saucer	$1.00	$40
2713	Set of 6 Egg Cups	$1.00	$40
2764	Tea Cup & Saucer	$1.10	$44
2876	Two Tier Tidbit	$5.00	$85
2905	Sugar & Creamer w/ Tray	$2.20	$55
2907	Cup & Saucer	$1.00	$40
2912	Sugar & Creamer	$0.55	$28
2913	Stacking Teapot Creamer & Sugar	$3.00	$120
2914	7" Three Compartment Dish	$2.50	$75
2917	Egg Cup	$0.50	$20
2918	8" Snack Set w/ Gold	$1.10	$44
2925	Salt & Pepper	$0.50	$20
2930	Sugar & Creamer	$1.10	$44
2934	AD Cup & Saucer	$1.10	$44
2992	10" Hors d'oeuvre Plate	$2.50	$100
2993	6" Tidbit Plate	$1.10	$44
2997	Tea Cup & Saucer	$1.10	$44
2999	8" Plate, match 2997	$1.10	$44
3166	Teapot	$2.00	$80
3167	Sugar & Creamer	$1.10	$44
3168	9" Plate	$0.60	$48
3170	Cup & Saucer	$0.60	$24
3647	8" Protestant Lord's Prayer Plate	$0.80	$32
3648	8" Catholic Lord's Prayer Plate	$0.80	$32
3925	Salt & Pepper	$0.50	$20
3928	Salt & Pepper	$1.00	$40
3819	Salt & Pepper	$0.60	$24
4044	6" Bone Dish	$0.25	$15
4046	6" Ashtray	$0.30	$15
4048	3 1/2" Egg Cup	$0.30	$15
4122	Nested Ashtray Set	$0.75	$30
4246	Cigarette Holder w/ 2 Trays	$0.55	$22
4814	4" Lattice Heart Shaped Trays	$0.75	$30
4829	Ribbed Teapot, Cream & Sugar Set	$2.25	$90
4911	2 1/2" 3 Piece Cigarette Set	$1.00	$40
4995	3" 5 Piece Stacking Ash Tray Set	$1.10	$44
6961	4" Protestant Bible Plaque	$0.40	$16
6962	4" Catholic Bible Plaque	$0.40	$16
9796	Cup & Saucer	$0.50	$32
9796	7 1/2" Rim Plate to match Cup & Saucer	$0.50	$32
9852	Two Tier Tidbit	$4.00	$85
20001	9" Plate, match 2997	$1.50	$48
20061	AD Cup & Saucer	$1.20	$35
20062	Cup w/ Lattice Saucer	$1.20	$35
20406	Compote	$0.60	$38
20610	4 Cup Teapot	$0.65	$75

ELEGANT VIOLET (Collector's Name) – 1952

		O.P.	C.B.V.
134	Cup & Saucer	$0.50	$32
134	7 1/2" Plate to match Cup & Saucer	$0.45	$30
134	9" Plate to Match Cup & Saucer	$0.60	$38
395	Stackable Sugar & Creamer	$0.55	$35
678	Cream & Sugar	$0.55	$22
702	Cream & Sugar w/ Twist Ribbing	$1.10	$44
885	Stacking Teapot Creamer & Sugar	$3.00	$120
934	Stacking Leaf Ashtrays, 3 in Set	$1.10	$44
958	Stacking Cream & Sugar	$1.50	$30
2033	7 1/2" Teapot	$2.50	$100
2124	8" Shell Shaped Snack Set	$1.10	$44
2125	Footed Cup & Saucer	$0.50	$32
2275	Ribbed Teapot	$1.50	$95

2276	Ribbed Cream & Sugar	$1.00	$40
2300	Ribbed Cup & Saucer	$1.00	$40
2300	Matching Ribbed Plate	$1.00	$40
2323	4 Cup Teapot w/ Swirl Pattern	$2.75	$110
2326	Sugar & Creamer	$1.10	$44
2328	Tea Cup & Saucer	$1.00	$40
2351	6" Three Section Tidbit Plate	$1.10	$44
2505	Sugar & Creamer	$1.00	$40
2562	9" Covered Candy Jar	$3.50	$140
2564	Stacking Sugar & Creamer	$1.50	$60
2565	4" Pitchers, 4 kinds	$1.10	$44
2736	Cup & Saucer	$1.00	$40
2713	Set of 6 Egg Cups	$1.00	440
2764	Tea Cup & Saucer	$1.10	$44
2872	8" Leaf Shape Nappy Dish	$1.50	$60
2874	8" Square Nappy Dish	$1.50	$60
2876	Two Tier Tidbit	$5.00	$85
2905	Sugar & Creamer w/ Tray	$2.20	$55
2912	Sugar & Creamer	$0.55	$28
2913	Stacking Teapot Creamer & Sugar	$3.00	$120
2914	7" Three Compartment Dish	$2.50	$75
2917	Egg Cup	$0.50	$20
2918	8" Snack Set w/ Gold	$1.10	$44
2925	Salt & Pepper	$0.50	$20
2930	Sugar & Creamer	$1.10	$44
2934	AD Cup & Saucer	$1.10	$44
2993	6" Tidbit Plate	$1.10	$44
2996	Cup & Saucer	$1.10	$44
2998	8" Plate, match 2996	$1.10	$44
3166	Teapot	$2.00	$80
3167	Sugar & Creamer	$1.10	$44
3168	9" Plate	$0.60	$48
3170	Cup & Saucer	$0.60	$24
3647	8" Protestant Lord's Prayer Plate	$0.80	$32
3648	8" Catholic Lord's Prayer Plate	$0.80	$32
3925	Salt & Pepper	$0.50	$20
3928	Salt & Pepper	$1.00	$40
3819	Salt & Pepper	$0.60	$24
4044	6" Bone Dish	$0.25	$15
4046	6" Ashtray	$0.30	$15
4048	3 1/2" Egg Cup	$0.30	$15
4814	4" Lattice Heart Shaped Trays	$0.75	$30
4829	Ribbed Teapot, Cream & Sugar Set	$2.25	$90
4911	2 1/2" 3 Piece Cigarette Set	$1.00	$40
4995	3" 5 Piece Stacking Ash Tray Set	$1.10	$44
6961	4" Protestant Bible Plaque	$0.40	$16
6962	4" Catholic Bible Plaque	$0.40	$16
9796	Cup & Saucer	$0.50	$32
9796	7 1/2" Rim Plate to match		
	Cup & Saucer	$0.50	$32
9852	Two Tier Tidbit	$4.00	$85
20000	9" Plate, match 2996	$1.50	$48
20053	7 1/4" Compote	$0.60	$38
20061	AD Cup & Saucer	$1.20	$35
20062	Cup w/ Lattice Saucer	$1.20	$35
20406	Compote	$0.60	$38
20610	4 Cup Teapots	$0.65	$75

ELF HEAD – 1967

		O.P.	C.B.V.
3968	Salt & Pepper	$0.75	$65
3969	Cookie Jar	$2.50	$225
3970	Sugar & Creamer	$1.50	$95

3971	Jam Jar w/ Spoon	$0.80	$75
3972	Wall Pocket	$0.80	$120
3973	Teapot	$1.50	$225

ESPRESSO – 1962

		O.P.	C.B.V.
2990	Cups & Saucers, 4 colors	$0.55	$15
2991	4 1/2" Ashtrays, 4 colors	$0.25	$10
3156	Tangerine Coffee Pot	$3.00	$65
3157	Sandalwood Coffee Pot	$3.00	$65
3159	Wisteria Coffee Pot	$3.00	$65
3160	Tangerine Sugar & Creamer	$1.10	$25
3161	Sandalwood Sugar & Creamer	$1.10	$25
3162	Wisteria Sugar & Creamer	$1.20	$25
3165	5" Ashtrays, 4 colors	$0.30	$10
3247	Tangerine Snack Set	$0.65	$18
3248	Sandalwood Snack Set	$0.65	$18
3249	Wisteria Snack Set	$0.65	$18
3283	7 1/2" Plate, 3 colors	$0.40	$15
3284	9" Plate, 3 colors	$0.60	$18
3250	Tangerine Cup & Saucer	$0.55	$15
3251	Sandalwood Cup & Saucer	$0.55	$15
3252	Wisteria Cup & Saucer	$0.55	$15
3408	4 1/2" Wisteria Cup & Saucer	$0.50	$15
3409	4 1/2" Sandalwood Cup & Saucer	$0.50	$15
3410	4 1/2" Tangerine Cup & Saucer	$0.50	$15

FESTIVAL – 1964

		O.P.	C.B.V.
2613	Teapot	$1.75	$145
2615	Sugar & Creamer	$1.00	$55
2616	Cup & Saucer	$0.65	$28
2617	Jam Jar w/ Plate & Spoon	$1.10	$50
2619	Tea & Toast	$0.80	$25
2620	7" Plate	$0.55	$18
2621	9" Plate	$0.80	$28
2622	AD Cup & Saucer	$0.45	$35
2624	Two Tier Tidbit Tray	$3.00	$85
2626	Salt & Pepper	$0.55	$25
2627	8 1/4" Bone Dish	$0.55	$15
2630	3 1/2" 8 Piece coaster set	$1.75	$48
2632	Candy Dish, 3 shapes	$0.65	$25
2935	Coffee Pot	$2.00	$155

FIESTA – 1968

		O.P.	C.B.V.
5254	Canister Set	$7.50	$120
5256	Cookie Jar	$3.25	$65
5278	14" Two Compartment Dish	$2.10	$42
5280	18" Three Compartment Dish	$4.50	$85
5281	6" Salt & Pepper	$1.35	$27
5282	6" Instant Coffee Jar w/ Spoon	$1.10	$22
5283	5" Jam Jar w/ Spoon	$1.00	$20
5291	9" Plate	$1.20	$24
5292	7" Pitcher	$1.50	$30
5293	8 1/2" Pitcher	$2.75	$55
5349	5" Mug	$0.75	$15
5379	7" Spoon Rest	$1.00	$20
5409	14" Egg Plate w/ Salt & Pepper	$2.50	$50

FLEUR DE LIS – 1959

		O.P.	C.B.V.
1028	4 Piece Cigarette Set	$2.00	$50

1044	4" Tumbler	$0.60	$15
1045	5 1/2" Soap Dish	$0.75	$18
1047	6" Tray	$0.75	$18
1048	3 1/2" Lipstick Holder	$0.65	$16
1049	4" Egg Shaped Box	$0.60	$15
1050	3 3/4" Box w/ Metal Rim	$1.50	$37
1800	Sugar & Creamer	$0.80	$20
1801	9" Snack Set	$0.65	$18
2123	5" Cigarette Set	$0.75	$18
2124	Nesting Ashtrays Square	$0.65	$16
2125	Nesting Ashtray Set	$0.55	$14
2356	8" Latticed Bowl	$0.55	$15
2797	Tumbler & Soap Dish	$0.65	$16
2904	3 3/4" 7 Piece Coaster Set	$1.50	$37
2909	3 1/2" Sugar & Creamer	$1.10	$27
2910	Coffee Pot	$1.75	$45
2911	Candy Box	$1.35	$32
3004	2 3/4" Sugar & Creamer	$0.60	$16

FLORAL BOUQUET – 1972

		O.P.	C.B.V.
7117	Service Set Coffee Pot	$3.25	$60
7117	Service Set Cream & Sugar	$1.75	$30
7117	Service Set Cup & Saucer	$1.00	$18
7157	5 3/4" Jam Jar	$1.25	$22
7159	6" Heart Shaped Candy Box	$2.25	$38
7160	7" Bud Vase, 3 shapes	$1.10	$20
7161	3" Fruit Shaped Ashtray, 3 kinds	$1.75	$30
7162	Pin Boxes	$0.70	$12
7163	6" Candy Dish, 2 shapes	$1.10	$20
7164	6 1/4" Candy Dish	$1.50	$24
7165	6 1/4" Ashtray, 2 shapes	$1.75	$23
7166	5 1/2" Footed Soap Dish	$1.50	$27
7254	Pitcher & Bowl	$1.75	$32
7255	Pitcher & Bowl	$3.00	$54
7300	3 1/2" Bell	$0.75	$14
7311	Pin Boxes, 3 kinds	$0.55	$10

FLORAL CHINTZ – 1973

		O.P.	C.B.V.
8033	9" Coffee Pot	$4.75	$150
8034	4" Sugar & Creamer	$1.75	$56
8035	2 1/4" Cup & Saucer	$1.75	$56
8036	7" Plate	$1.00	$32
8037	9" Plate	$1.65	$50
8038	6 1/4" Pitcher w/ Bowl	$6.25	$200
8039	5 1/4" Pitcher w/ Bowl	$4.25	$135
8040	3 1/4" Pitcher w/ Bowl	$2.00	$64
8041	6 1/2" Nappy Dish, 3 kinds	$1.50	$48
8042	4 1/2" Candy Box	$2.50	$80
8043	7" Compote	$1.75	$56

FORGET-ME-NOT – 1966

		O.P.	C.B.V.
4174	Coffee Pot	$2.00	$70
4175	Sugar & Creamer	$1.50	$50
4176	Teapot	$2.00	$70
4177	Cup & Saucer	$0.65	$25
4178	AD Cup & Saucer	$0.55	$20
4179	Tea & Toast Set	$1.00	$35
4180	7" Plate	$0.55	$20
4181	9" Plate	$1.00	$35
4182	Two Tier Tidbit Tray	$3.00	$65

4183	Candy Box	$1.75	$55
4184	Salt & Pepper	$0.50	$20
4185	Jam Jar w/ Plate & Spoon	$1.25	$40
4186	6 1/4" Bone Dish	$0.50	$16
4187	6" Nappy Dish	$0.75	$24
4188	Tumble Up	$2.50	$85
4189	5 1/2" Pitcher 7 1/4" Bowl	$2.00	$60
4190	6 1/4" Pitcher 9 1/4" Bowl	$3.00	$55

FRENCH ROSE – 1965

		O.P.	C.B.V.
2633	5" Soap Dish	$0.80	$20
2634	3 3/4" Tumbler	$0.55	$14
2640	3 3/4" Ring Holder	$0.55	$14
2642	4 1/2" Covered Jar	$0.55	$14
2646	3 3/4" Toothbrush Holder	$0.75	$18
2648	3 1/2" Lipstick Holder	$0.60	$15
2649	3 Piece Perfume Set	$2.00	$50
2651	6 1/4" Bud Vase, 3 shapes	$0.50	$13
2652	4" Denture Box "His"	$0.80	$20
2653	4" Denture Box "Hers"	$0.80	$20
2654	Pin Box, 3 shapes	$0.30	$10
2656	3 1/2" Cigarette Urn w/ 2 Trays	$1.10	$27
3202	4 1/2" Tile Trivet	$0.65	$17
3203	6" Tile Trivet	$1.25	$28
3216	Pin Tray, 4 shapes	$0.80	$20
3232	Jam Jar w/ Spoon	$0.80	$20
3253	Oval Pin Box	$0.40	$10
3263	4 3/4" Combination Covered Box	$1.00	$20
3294	3" Tile Trivet	$0.40	$10
3381	3 1/2" Lipstick Holder	$0.55	$14
3382	Cigarette Set w/ 2 Trays	$1.25	$28
3383	3 1/2" Pitcher & 5" Bowl	$1.10	$27
3384	Three Piece Perfume Set	$1.50	$38
3385	3" Candleholder, Pair	$0.80	$20
3386	5 1/2" Covered Jar	$0.75	$17
3387	3 1/2" Covered Jar	$0.40	$10
3390	6 1/2" Soap Dish	$0.80	$20
3391	2 3/4" Purse Planter, 3 kinds	$0.25	$13
3392	Sugar & Creamer	$0.65	$18
3393	2 1/4" Match Box	$0.20	$10
3395	Pin Box, 4 kinds	$0.30	$10
3448	Teapot	$2.25	$55
3449	Sugar & Creamer	$1.50	$35
3450	AD Cup & Saucer	$0.55	$15
3451	Cup & Saucer	$0.65	$16
3452	7 1/2" Plate	$0.60	$15
3455	9" Plate	$1.00	$25
3483	Salt & Pepper	$0.50	$13
3484	3 3/4" Nappy Dish	$0.65	$16
3548	4 3/4" Pin Dish	$0.30	$10
3600	3 1/2" Ashtrays, Set of 4	$0.80	$20
3834	Tape Dispenser & Stamp Box	$1.10	$28
3835	7 Piece Cigarette Set	$1.75	$42
4035	Snack Set	$0.75	$18
4063	2 Cup Teapot	$0.60	$35
4071	2 3/4" Sugar & Creamer, 2 shapes	$0.65	$20
4100	Tumbler & Soap Dish	$1.00	$25

FRUIT BASKET (Tutti Fruit Label) – 1959

		O.P.	C.B.V.
1657	Salt & Pepper	$0.50	$20
1658	Two Compartment Dish	$1.00	$40

1659	Three Compartment Dish	$1.25	$50
1662	Four Compartment Dish	$1.50	$60
1663	Bonbon Dish	$0.55	$22
1665	Egg Tray	$1.50	$60
1666	Butter Dish	$0.75	$30
1667	Sugar & Creamer	$1.00	$40
1668	Tea Pot	$1.50	$60
1669	Condiment Set	$1.00	$40
1670	Large Pitcher	$1.50	$60
1671	Medium Pitcher	$1.00	$40
1672	Wall Plaque, Pair	$1.25	$50
1673	Oil & Vinegar	$1.00	$40
1674	Cookie Jar	$2.00	$80
1675	Candy Box	$1.50	$60
1676	Four Piece Canister Set	$4.50	$145
1677	Cigarette Set	$1.10	$44
1678	Compote	$1.25	$50
1679	Egg Cup	$0.30	$18
1681	Three Compartment Dish	$1.25	$50
1680	Jam Jar	$0.75	$30
1682	10 1/2" Salad Bowl w/ Fork & Spoon	$2.00	$80
1890	Candle Holders, Pair	$1.00	$40
1891	Chip & Dip	$2.00	$80
1892	Jardiniere	$0.65	$26
1893	Plate w/ Handle	$0.80	$32
1894	12" Celery Tray	$1.00	$40
1895	Tea Bag Holder	$0.25	$10
1896	Two Tier Tidbit Tray	$1.80	$70
1952	Spoon Rest	$0.50	$20
1983	9" Plate	$0.60	$28
1984	Cup & Saucer	$0.55	$25
1990	Mug	$0.50	$20

FRUIT DELIGHT (Collector's Name) – 1965

		O.P.	C.B.V.
2548	12 1/2" Candy Box	$4.80	$95
3131	6 Cup Tea Pot	$2.25	$70
3132	Cream & Sugar	$1.25	$35
3133	5" Jam Jar	$0.80	$20

FRUIT FANTASIA – 1971

		O.P.	C.B.V.
6721	Canister Set	$10.00	$15.00
6722	Cookie Jar	$4.00	$60
6723	8 1/2" Spoon Rest	$1.10	$17
6724	Covered Butter Dish	$1.75	$26
6725	5 1/4" Pitcher	$2.10	$32
6726	5 1/2" Pitcher w/ Bowl	$2.75	$42
6727	5 1/2" Jam Jar	$1.25	$24
6728	5 1/2" Napkin Holder	$1.75	$18
6729	Two Tier Tidbit Tray	$4.50	$65
6730	3 1/2" Mug	$0.90	$13
6731	9 1/4" Plate	$1.75	$26
6732	Snack Set	$2.75	$38
6754	6 3/4" Salt & Pepper	$1.75	$24
6755	Teapot	$3.00	$65
6756	Sugar & Creamer	$2.10	$30
6776	9 1/4" Egg Platter w/ Salt & Pepper	$3.00	$45

FRUITS OF ITALY – 1963

		O.P.	C.B.V.
621	Cookie Jar -	$2.50	$60
623	Jam Jar w/ Plate & Spoon	$1.00	$25

1175	Coffee Pot	$2.25	$65
1177	Sugar & Creamer	$1.25	$30
1178	9 1/2" Two Compartment Dish	$1.10	$27
1179	9 1/4" Three Compartment Dish	$1.75	$43
1205	Compote	$1.75	$43
1207	Salt & Pepper Shaker	$0.60	$15
1208	6 1/2" Pitcher	$1.10	$27
1209	3 1/2" Mug	$0.55	$13
1211	11 1/4" x 7 1/4" Tray	$1.35	$34
1212	Two Tier Tidbit Tray	$2.10	$50
1334	8 1/2" Plate or Wall Plaque	$1.00	$25
1335	6" Candy Box	$1.50	$38

GARDEN BOUQUET – 1965

		O.P.	C.B.V.
1889	Pin Box	$0.30	$21
3475	Teapot	$2.25	$160
3476	Sugar & Creamer	$1.50	$65
3477	AD Cup & Saucer	$0.55	$38
3478	Cup & Saucer	$0.65	$45
3479	7 1/2" Plate	$0.60	$38
3480	9" Plate	$1.00	$45
3481	Salt & Pepper	$0.50	$35
3482	7 3/4" Nappy Dish	$0.65	$40

GARDEN BOUQUET – 1979

		O.P.	C.B.V.
1892	2" Pin Box	$1.25	$9
1893	3" Pin Box	$1.75	$12
1894	4" Covered Box	$4.25	$30
1895	6 Napkin Rings	$6.50	$45
1896	2 1/2" Pin Box	$2.50	$17
1897	4" Covered Box	$4.00	$28
1898	3" Pin Box	$1.50	$10
1899	4 3/4" Frame	$3.00	$21
1900	7" Frame	$8.00	$45
1901	2 1/2" Pin Box	$2.25	$15
1902	5 1/2" Covered Box	$5.00	$35
1903	5" Soap Dish	$2.50	$17
1904	5" Mirror	$2.10	$15
1905	12 1/2" Platter	$8.50	$60
1906	9 1/4" Cake Plate	$5.00	$35
1907	5 1/2" Compote	$4.25	$30
1908	4 1/2" Candy Box	$4.50	$31
1909	6 1/4" Vase, 3 kinds	$2.25	$16
1910	2" Pin Box	$1.35	$10
1911	2" Pin Box	$1.25	$9
1912	2 1/2" Pin Box	$2.00	$14
1913	9 1/4" Tray	$3.50	$25
1914	3 1/4" Pitcher w/ Bowl	$2.50	$17
1916	4" Tumbler	$2.25	$16
1917	6" Nappy Dish	$3.00	$21
1921	5" Dish	$2.75	$19
1922	3 1/4" Bell	$2.00	$14
1923	4" Toothbrush Holder	$2.75	$19
2157	3" Pin Box, 4 kinds	$2.00	$14
2213	3 1/2" Shopping Bag Planter	$3.00	$21
2288	8 1/2" Pen Tray	$2.25	$16
2460	7" Vase	$2.00	$14
2524	3 3/4" Purse Planter	$3.00	$21
8312	5 3/4" Leaf Shaped Dish	$2.00	$14
01892	2" Pin Box	$1.25	$9
01894	4" Covered Box	$4.25	$30

01895	6 Napkin Rings	$6.50	$45
01896	2 1/2" Pin Box	$2.50	$17
01898	3" Pin Box	$1.50	$10
01899	4 3/4" Frame	$3.00	$21
01900	7" Frame	$8.00	$45
01901	2 1/2" Pin Box	$2.25	$15
01902	5 1/2" Covered Box	$5.00	$35
01903	5" Soap Dish	$2.50	$17
01906	9 1/4" Cake Plate	$5.00	$35
01907	5 1/2" Compote	$4.25	$30
01908	4 1/2" Candy Box	$4.50	$31
01909	6 1/4" Vase, 3 kinds	$2.25	$16
01911	2" Pin Box	$1.25	$9
01912	2 1/2" Pin Box	$2.00	$14
01913	9 1/4" Tray	$3.50	$25
01914	3 1/4" Pitcher w/ Bowl	$2.50	$17
01916	4" Tumbler	$2.25	$16
01917	6" Nappy Dish	$3.00	$16
01921	5" Dish	$2.75	$19
01922	3 1/4" Bell	$2.00	$14
01923	4" Toothbrush Holder	$2.75	$19
02034	2 1/2" AD Cup & Saucer	$2.50	$18
02213	3 1/2" Shopping Bag Planter	$3.00	$21
02288	8 1/2" Pen Tray	$2.25	$16
02460	7" Vase	$2.00	$14
02524	3 3/4" Purse Planter	$3.00	$21
02611	3 1/2" Egg Cup	$2.00	$14
02656	3" Tea Strainer	$2.00	$14
02677	3" Dish	$1.75	$12
02767	4" Box	$3.50	$25
02770	2 1/2" Salt & Pepper Shaker	$3.00	$21
RE2823	5" Jewel Box	$7.50	$45
02832	6 1/2" Vase	$4.00	$28
02838	4 1/2" Bell	$3.75	$22
02852	8 3/4" Vase	$7.50	$52
02898	4 1/2" Toothpick Holder	$2.75	$19
02908	6 1/2" Vase	$3.00	$21
02955	4 3/4" Ginger Jar	$4.50	$31
02960	6" Temple Jar	$4.50	$31
02969	5" Dish	$2.50	$18
03024	4" Footed Mug	$2.50	$17
03038	7" Picture Frame	$9.00	$45
03040	4 3/4" Picture Frame	$5.00	$21
04832	3" Ring Holder	$2.50	$12
06004	8 3/4" Cylinder Shape Vase	$8.00	$32
07809	2 1/4" Egg Salt & Pepper Shakers	$2.50	$12
07833	2 1/2" Egg Cup	$1.75	$9
07838	3" Egg Box	$2.75	$19
07839	2" Egg Box	$2.00	$14
08282	5" Tea Bag Holder	$1.75	$12
08312	5 3/4" Leaf Shaped Dish	$2.00	$14

GARDEN DAISY – 1978

		O.P.	C.B.V.
1501	Canister Set	$30.00	$95
1502	Cookie Jar	$11.00	$58
1503	3 Quart Soup Tureen w/ Tray & Ladle	$30.00	$85
1504	10" Egg Plate	$3.50	$25
1505	3 3/4" Sugar & Creamer	$4.50	$30
1506	8" Coffee Pot	$5.75	$40
1507	6" Salt & Pepper	$3.00	$21
1508	4 1/4" Jam Jar	$2.50	$18
1509	12" Chip & Dip Set	$8.50	$60
1510	12" Four Compartment Dish	$7.75	$55
1511	8 1/2" Planter	$5.00	$28
1512	5" Napkin Holder	$2.75	$20
1561	4 1/2" Cache Pot	$2.50	$18
8262	4 1/2" Mug	$1.35	$10

GINGHAM – 1962
Tan & Apricot

		O.P.	C.B.V.
3265	Coffee Pot	$2.00	$65
3266	Sugar & Creamer	$1.10	$25
3267	Cup & Saucer	$0.60	$20
3268	9 1/4" Plate	$0.60	$20
3297	Tea & Toast Set	$0.80	$28
3298	Mug	$0.35	$12
3299	6 3/4" Oil & Vinegar	$1.25	$42
3300	Egg Cup	$0.30	$10
3301	Covered Butter Dish	$0.75	$26
3302	Jam Jar w/ Plate & Spoon	$0.80	$28
3326	17 Piece Tea Set	$6.60	$230
3333	Cookie Jar	$2.00	$65
3336	Salt & Pepper Shakers	$0.60	$21

Light Purple & Blue/Grey

		O.P.	C.B.V.
3273	Coffee Pot	$2.00	$65
3274	Sugar & Creamer	$1.10	$25
3275	Cup & Saucer	$0.60	$20
3276	9 1/4" Plate	$0.60	$20
3309	Tea & Toast Set	$0.80	$28
3310	Mug	$0.35	$12
3311	6 3/4" Oil & Vinegar	$1.25	$41
3312	Egg Cup	$0.30	$10
3313	Covered Butter Dish	$0.75	$26
3314	Jam Jar w/ Plate & Spoon	$0.80	$28
3328	17 Piece Tea Set	$6.60	$230
3335	Cookie Jar	$2.00	$65
3338	Salt & Pepper Shakers	$0.60	$21

Tan & Misty Green

		O.P.	C.B.V.
3269	Coffee Pot	$2.00	$65
3270	Sugar & Creamer	$1.10	$25
3271	Cup & Saucer	$0.60	$20
3272	9 1/4" Plate	$0.60	$20
3303	Tea & Toast Set	$0.80	$28
3304	Mug	$0.35	$12
3305	6 3/4" Oil & Vinegar	$1.25	$41
3306	Egg Cup	$0.30	$10
3307	Covered Butter Dish	$0.75	$26
3308	Jam Jar w/ Plate & Spoon	$0.80	$28
3327	17 Piece Tea Set	$6.60	$230
3334	Cookie Jar	$2.00	$65
3337	Salt & Pepper Shakers	$0.60	$21

GOLDEN FLOWER (Collector's Name) – 1959

		O.P.	C.B.V.
237	Snack Set	$0.65	$23
238	Sugar & Creamer	$1.00	$35
239	6 Cup Tea Pot	$1.25	$45

GOLDEN LAUREL – 1961

		O.P.	C.B.V.
2310	2" Pin Boxes, 3 kinds	$0.30	$10
2311	2" Postage Stamp Box	$0.35	$12
2398	13 3/4" Tray	$3.50	$85
2399	4 1/2" Perfume Atomizer	$0.80	$20
2400	3 3/4" Jewel Box	$1.25	$30
2401	Three Piece Perfume Set	$2.50	$63
2402	9 1/4" Mirror	$2.50	$63
2403	4" Tumbler	$0.60	$15
2404	Three Piece Bathroom Set	$2.00	$50
2405	5 1/2" Soap Dish	$0.75	$18
2406	6" Ashtray	$0.80	$20
2407	5 3/4" Covered Urn	$1.00	$25
2408	9" Oval Tray	$1.50	$38
2409	4 1/4" Cigarette Box w/ 2 Trays	$2.50	$45
2410	Four Piece Cigarette Set	$2.50	$45
2411	2 1/2" Covered Box	$0.60	$15
2412	7" Covered Urn	$1.50	$38
2413	2 3/4" Salt & Pepper w/ Metal Tops	$0.33	$12
2414	3 1/4" Lipstick Holder	$0.60	$15
2426	6" Teapot	$1.50	$65
2427	Sugar & Creamer	$0.80	$26
2428	2 3/4" Salt & Pepper	$0.33	$10
2442	Two Tier Tidbit Tray	$1.50	$65
2525	6 1/2" Three Piece Cigarette Set	$1.00	$25
2526	7 1/2" Candy Box on Tray	$2.00	$50
2527	5 1/2" Candy Box	$1.25	$38
2528	6 1/2" Candy Box	$0.80	$26
2529	4 1/2" Jam Jar w/ Spoon	$0.80	$26
2530	6 1/2" Bone Dish	$0.35	$10
2531	8 1/2" Dish	$0.60	$15
2532	6" Dish w/ Handle	$0.40	$10
2533	6" Fruit Dish	$0.60	$15
2548	Cup & Saucer	$0.55	$20
2549	Cup & Saucer	$0.40	$18
2550	9 1/4" Latticed Compote	$3.00	$65
2591	8" Plate	$0.45	$14
2592	9" Plate	$0.60	$20
2597	8" Snack Set	$0.65	$22
2598	9" Snack Set	$0.82	$25
2624	Compote	$0.65	$18

GOLD LEAF – 1964

		O.P.	C.B.V.
923	Cigarette Set w/ 2 Trays	$1.00	$20
2472	6 1/2" Candy Box, 2 kinds	$2.00	$40
3342	Teapot	$1.50	$42
3365	Sugar & Creamer	$1.10	$22
3366	7 1/2" Plate	$0.60	$12
3367	Cup & Saucer	$0.65	$14
3368	5 1/2" Dish	$0.50	$10
3374	3 1/2" Cigarette Set w/ 2 Trays	$0.65	$13
3375	3 3/4" Pin Box	$0.80	$16
3549	6 1/4" Candy Box	$3.00	$60

GOLDEN ROSE (Collector's Name) – 1959

		O.P.	C.B.V.
1406	6 Cup Tea Pot	$1.25	$45
1407	Sugar & Creamer	$0.80	$35
1408	8" Snack Set	$0.55	$22
1409	8" Plate	$0.45	$15
1410	Cup & Saucer	$0.50	$14
1413	7 1/2" Double Bonbon	$0.75	$21
1414	Compote	$0.60	$18

GOLDEN TREE – 1959

		O.P.	C.B.V.
1872	Three Compartment Dish w/ Handle	$2.75	$75
1873	Coffee Pot	$2.75	$75
1874	Sugar & Creamer	$1.50	$40
1875	Two-Tier Tidbit Tray	$5.00	$75
1876	Snack Set	$0.55	$18
1877	Miniature Cream & Sugar	$1.10	$30
1878	Teapot	$2.50	$68
1879	Nesting Ashtrays	$0.55	$18
1880	Creamer & Sugar	$1.50	$40

GOLDEN WHEAT – 1955

		O.P.	C.B.V.
112	7" Compote	$0.60	$32
875	Cigarette Box w/ 2 Trays	$0.65	$16
888	5 1/2" Instant Coffee Jar	$0.75	$28
1428	10" Plate	$1.00	$25
1926	Sugar & Creamer	$0.80	$20
2045	7" Lattice Dish	$0.60	$15
2568	Coffee Pot	$2.75	$68
2606	9" Covered Candy Jar	$5.00	$75
2743	6 5/8" Butter Dish	$0.65	$20
2768	8" Snack Set	$0.55	$13
2769	9" Snack Set	$0.75	$18
2869	Cup & Saucer	$1.20	$16
2870	Reticulated Cup & Saucer	$1.00	$15
2871	Demi Cup & Saucer, 2 kinds	$0.80	$20
2876	Two Tier Tidbit Tray	$5.00	$45
4849	2 1/2" 3 Piece Cigarette Set, 3 kinds	$1.00	$25
6607	11" Overall Lavabo	$12.00	$85
20120	Sugar & Creamer	$1.10	$27
20121	Egg Cup	$0.30	$12
20122	5" Stacking Cream & Sugar	$1.60	$48
20124	4 Nesting Trays	$0.55	$13
21025	Coaster	$0.30	$10
20126	Two Tier Tidbit Tray	$5.00	$45
20182	Tea Pot (1956)	$1.25	$68
20183	Sugar & Creamer	$1.50	$37
20191	6" Covered Candy Box	$1.00	$25
20197	9" Double Bonbon	$1.00	$25
20198	5" Candle Holder, Pair	$2.00	$32
20230	8" Meat Plate	$0.45	$14
20231	Single Tidbit Tray	$0.65	$16
20312	6" Bonbon	$0.80	$20
20313	9" Triple Bonbon	$1.75	$42
20314	5" Covered Candy, 2 Colors	$1.75	$42
20316	9" 3 Piece Console Set, 2 Colors	$3.00	$65
20317	7" Vases, 2 shapes	$1.25	$30
20560	3 Piece Tea Set, Coffee, Cream, Sugar	$2.00	$85
20590	Coffee Pot	$2.00	$68
20595	Sugar & Creamer	$1.10	$28
20602/9	9" Plate	$0.60	$18
20602	Cup & Saucer	$0.50	$15
30119	Salt & Pepper	$0.30	$10
30158	Salt & Pepper, 2 kinds	$1.00	$25
40123	7" Ash Tray	$0.50	$12
40124	3" Nesting Ashtrays, Round	$1.10	$26
40124	3" Nesting Ashtrays, Square	$1.10	$26

40154	8" Ash Tray	$1.20	$26
40190	5" 3 Piece Cigarette Set	$1.00	$25
40613	8" 3 Piece Cigarette Set	$2.00	$42
50561	8 1/2" Violin Planter	$0.55	$14
70315	5" Vase, 3 kinds	$0.55	$14
70317	7" Vase, 2 shapes Left & Right	$0.80	$20
90198	5" Candlesticks, Pair	$1.00	$25

GRAPE LINE – 1963

		O.P.	C.B.V.
152	4 Piece Measuring Cup Set	$0.60	$85
639	5 3/4" Candy Box	$1.25	$65
640	10" Two Compartment Dish	$1.10	$56
641	6 1/2" Pitcher	$1.25	$65
642	8" Plate	$0.75	$39
643	2 3/4" Salt & Pepper	$0.60	$32
644	9 1/2" Three Compartment Dish	$1.75	$85
1230	7 3/4" Pitcher	$1.75	$85
2663	Teapot	$1.80	$90
2664	Sugar & Creamer	$1.75	$50
2665	10" Tray	$0.65	$48
3023	4 1/2" Jam Jar	$0.85	$45
3319	7" Cookie Jar	$2.25	$125

GREEN HERITAGE, EARLY (Collector's Name) – 1958

		O.P.	C.B.V.
510	Coffee Pot	$2.00	$175
511	Sugar & Creamer	$1.00	$75
512	Cup & Saucer	$0.55	$40
513	9" Plate	$0.65	$65
514	7 1/2" Plate	$0.45	$45

GREEN HERITAGE – 1962

		O.P.	C.B.V.
719	9 1/4" Plate (1965-1980)	$1.25	$60
731	3 1/4" Pitchers, 3 kinds (1963-1978)	$0.40	$24
748	5 1/2" Vases, 3 kinds (1963-1984)	$0.60	$32
792	Teapot (1965-1984)	$3.00	$165
796	6 1/2" Pitcher (1965-1980)	$2.50	$95
1150	2 Cup Teapot (1962–1963)	$0.75	$95
1151	Cup & Saucer (1963-1984)	$0.85	$32
1152	4 1/2" Jam Jar w/ Plate & Spoon (1963-1980)	$0.45	$50
1153	Two Tier Tidbit Tray (1963-1980)	$3.00	$85
1266	Tumble Up (1963-1980)	$2.50	$85
1274	Compote (1963-1967)	$1.00	$60
1860	7" Nappy Dish, 3 kinds (1965-1980)	$0.65	$35
2274	7" Compote (1966-1980)	$1.00	$48
3065	8 Cup Coffee Pot (1962-1980)	$3.00	$125
3066	4 1/2" Sugar & Creamer (1962-1980)	$1.75	$55
3067	Cup & Saucer (1962-1980)	$1.10	$40
3068	7 1/4" Plate (1962-1980)	$0.60	$35
3069	9" Plate (1962-1980)	$1.00	$48
3070	2 1/2" Salt & Pepper (1962-1980)	$0.45	$30
3071	8" Snack Set (1962-1980)	$0.80	$38
3708	6 1/2" Bone Dish (1965-1979)	$0.45	$28
4053	4 1/2" Candy Box (1966-1980)	$1.50	$50
4072	8 3/4" Vase, 3 kinds (1966-1980)	$2.00	$68
4169	11" Oil Lamp (1966-1975)	$2.00	$150
4171	13" Oil Lamp (1966-1972)	$4.00	$225
4172	5 1/2" Pitcher w/ 7" Bowl (1966–1974)	$2.20	$125
4577	3 1/4" Pitcher w/ 4 1/2" Bowl (1967-1980)	$1.00	$60
4578	5 1/4" Pitcher w/ 7 1/4" Bowl (1967–1980)	$2.25	$135
4579	6 1/4" Pitcher & 9" Bowl (1970-1980)	$3.75	$200
4938	Sugar & Creamer (1969)	$2.10	$125
4998	4 1/2" Invalid Pitcher (1968-1969)	$1.00	$95
5242	12" Electric Lamp (1970)	$5.00	$300
5243	11" Electric Lamp (1970-1971)	$3.50	$210
5586	7" Pitcher (1969)	$3.00	$180
5680	Cup & Saucer (1971-1980)	$1.25	$45
6131	6 1/2" Candy Box (1971-1980)	$4.50	$175
6710	2 Cup Teapot (1971-1978)	$2.00	$65
7543	9 1/2" Musical Teapot "Tea For Two" (1973)	$5.50	$85

GREEN HERITAGE – 1981

		O.P.	C.B.V.
00719	9 1/4" Cake Plate (1981-1986)	$8.00	$48
00748	5 1/2" Vase, 3 kinds (1981-1986)	$4.00	$24
00792	8" Teapot (1981-1986)	$18.00	$108
00796	6 1/2" Pitcher (1981-1982)	$13.00	$78
01151	2 1/4" AD Cup & Saucer (1981-1986)	$1.95	$22
01152	4" Jam Jar w/ Plate & Spoon (1981-1982)	$6.00	$36
01153	11" Two Tier Tidbit Tray (1981-1986)	$15.00	$75
01266	Tumble-Up (1981-1986)	$15.00	$75
01860	6" Nappy Dish, 3 kinds (1981-1986)	$4.25	$25
02274	7" Compote (1981-1986)	$8.00	$24
03065	8 3/4" Coffee Pot (1981-1986)	$18.00	$110
03066	4 1/2" Sugar & Creamer (1981-1986)	$15.00	$55
03067	3" Cup & Saucer (1981-1986)	$7.00	$35
03068	7 1/4" Plate (1981-1986)	$3.75	$32
03069	9" Plate (1981-1986)	$6.00	$42
03070	2 1/2" Salt & Pepper Shakers (1981-1986)	$4.50	$27
03071	8" Snack Set (1981-1986)	$7.50	$35
04072	8 3/4" Vase, 3 kinds (1981-1986)	$11.00	$65
04053	4 1/2" Candy Box (1981-1984)	$8.00	$48
04577	3 1/4" Pitcher w/ Bowl (1981-1986)	$6.00	$36
04578	5 1/4" Pitcher w/ Bowl (1981-1986)	$13.50	$80
04579	6 1/4" Pitcher w/ Bowl (1981-1982)	$16.00	$95
05680	2 1/4" Cup & Saucer (1981-1986)	$5.75	$35
06131	6 1/4" Candy Box (1981-1982)	$11.00	$95
07543	9 1/2" Musical Teapot (1987)	$15.00	$60

GREEN HERITAGE (Dated as early as 1984) – 1988

		O.P.	C.B.V.
05850	8 3/4" Coffee Pot (1988-1999)	$22.50	$90
05851	4 1/2" Sugar & Creamer (1988-1999)	$17.50	$45
05852	Cup & Saucer (1988-1999)	$8.50	$34
05853	AD Cup & Saucer (1987-1999)	$7.00	$28
05854	Cup & Saucer (1988-1999)	$7.50	$30
05855	7 1/4" Plate (1988-1999)	$5.00	$20
05856	9" Plate (1988-1999)	$7.50	$30
05857	Teapot (1988-1999)	$22.50	$90
05858	9" Cake Plate (1988-1999)	$10.00	$40
05860	5 1/2" Bud Vase, 3 kinds (1988-1993)	$5.50	$22
05861	8 3/4" Vase, 3 kinds (1988-1992)	$15.00	$60
05862	6 1/2" Dish, 3 kinds (1988-1993)	$5.00	$20
05863	6" Candle holder, Pair (1988-1992)	$8.50	$34
05864	6 1/2" Bud Vase, 3 Kinds (1988-1992)	$6.00	$24
06075	2 1/2" Salt & Pepper (1988-1999)	$6.50	$26

06076	5 1/2" Tumble-Up (1988-1993)	$15.00	$60
06077	7 1/2" Pitcher w/ Bowl (1988-1993)	$15.00	$60
06078	4 3/4" Pitcher w/ Bowl (1988-1995)	$8.00	$32
07543	9 1/2" Musical Teapot (1987-1997)	$17.50	$60

GREEN HERITAGE (Dated 1999) – 2000

		O.P.	C.B.V.
05850	Coffee Pot	$37.50	$75
05851	Sugar & Creamer	$32.50	$65
05852	Cup & Saucer	$13.50	$27
05853	AD Cup & Saucer	$12.00	$24
05854	5 1/2" Cup & Saucer	$13.00	$26
05855	7" Plate	$8.50	$17
05856	9" Plate	$13.50	$27
05057	Teapot	$37.50	$75
05858	9" Cake Plate	$17.50	$35
06075	2 1/2" Salt & Pepper	$11.00	$22
12367	6 1/2" Pitcher	$12.50	$25
12368	Teapot Teabag Holder	$3.50	$7
12369	Tray	$11.50	$23
12371	8" Vase	$16.50	$33
12374	10 1/2" Pedestal Cake Plate	$24.00	$48
12370	3" Basket	$5.00	$10
12378	Candleholder	$9.00	$18
12829	Covered Box, 3 kinds	$6.00	$12
12830	Compote	$10.00	$20
12831	Planter	$9.50	$19
12832	Oval Dish	$7.00	$14
12833	Leaf Dish	$7.50	$15

GREEN HOLLY/HOLLYBERRY – 1959

		O.P.	C.B.V.
158	5 1/4" Bell Bank	$1.10	$65
159	6" Candy Box	$1.25	$44
161	6" Plate	$0.45	$18
402	9" Pansy Ring, 2 Pieces	$2.20	$75
717	Candle Holder, Pair	$0.80	$28
787	Bell	$0.30	$10
807	10 1/2" Two Compartment Dish	$1.00	$35
876	8 1/2" Three Compartment Dish	$1.25	$44
1187	4" Reindeer	$0.55	$35
1346	Sleigh	$1.10	$38
1347	7 1/2" Ash Tray	$0.50	$15
1348	Celery Dish	$0.80	$28
1349	Two Compartment Dish	$1.00	$35
1351	Three Compartment Dish	$1.25	$45
1352	Four Compartment Dish	$1.50	$55
1353	Salt & Pepper	$0.50	$18
1355	Cream & Sugar	$1.00	$35
1357	Tea Pot	$1.50	$65
1359	Cookie Jar	$1.75	$70
1360	Candle Holders w/ climbers	$0.80	$28
1361	Candy Box	$0.80	$28
1362	Candy Dish	$2.00	$70
1363	Snack Set	$0.75	$27
1364	Two Tier Tidbit Tray	$3.00	$75
1365	Musical Hors d'oeuvre	$3.00	$75
1366	Mug	$0.30	$12
1367	Punch Bowl	$2.50	$85
1368	Reindeer Candle Holders, Pair	$1.50	$52
1693	3" Sleigh	$0.35	$18
2047	Cup & Saucer	$0.55	$20
2048	9" Plate	$0.60	$21

2217	12" Cake Plate	$4.20	$95
2272	Compote	$2.50	$65
2369	18" Platter	$3.50	$70
2620	7" Candleholder w/ Candle	$1.75	$48
2637	10" x 5 1/2" Sleigh	$2.00	$68
2688	11 3/4" Tree Shaped Dish	$1.25	$44
2691	8" Tree Shaped Dish	$0.60	$21
2692	10" Musical Lamp w/ Candle	$4.00	$125
2693	8 1/2" Vase	$2.00	$68
2694	8 1/2" Lamp w/ Candle	$2.10	$70
2695	9" Lamp w/ Bracket & Candle	$2.10	$70
2696	9 1/2" Planter w/ Bracket	$2.00	$68
3752	6" Candy Box	$1.25	$45
3854	14 3/4" Tree Shaped Serving Dish w/ Cover	$3.50	$70
4016	7 1/2" Hors d'oeuvres Tree	$2.00	$40
4017	6" Hors d'oeuvres Tree	$1.10	$22
4018	8" Musical Hors d'oeuvres Tree	$4.00	$80
4019	7" Tree Shaped Candy Box	$1.75	$35
4036	Tree Shaped Salt & Pepper	$0.60	$12
4229	5 3/4" Oil Lamp	$0.80	$16
4231	8" Compote	$1.75	$35
4284	3 1/2" Mug w/ Pixie Handle	$0.55	$11
4369	2" Candleholder w/ Candle	$0.45	$10
4621	5" Sleigh	$0.55	$18
4855	Candleholder w/ Candle set, 4 pieces	$4.00	$80
4858	9" Bell Shape Tray	$0.75	$15
4859	11 1/2" Bell Shape Tray	$1.50	$30
4863	7 1/4" Oil Lamp	$2.75	$85
4870	8 1/4" Pitcher	$2.25	$45
5171	9" Three Compartment Dish	$3.00	$60
5172	8" Two Compartment Dish	$1.35	$35
5173	6 Piece Hors d'oeuvres Set Inc. Plastic Tray	$5.00	$85
5174	4" Pitcher w/ 5 1/2" Bowl	$1.35	$27
5175	5 1/2" Bowl w/ Handle	$2.10	$42
5176	4 3/4" Bowl w/ Handle	$0.80	$16
5178	4" Cigarette Urn w/ 2 Ashtrays	$1.00	$20
5179	3 1/4" Shoe Salt & Pepper	$0.65	$13
5183	Mini Sugar & Creamer on Tray	$0.65	$13
5184	3 1/4" Shoe Planter	$0.60	$12
5185	4 3/4" Shoe Planter	$1.20	$24
5186	4 3/4" Bowl w/ Handle	$0.80	$16
5188	5 1/4" Pitcher w/ 7 1/4" Bowl	$2.25	$45
5189	Two Tier Bowl w/ Wooden Handle	$2.50	$50
5218	4 1/2" Reindeer	$0.75	$35
5563	11 1/2" Lighted Christmas Tree	$5.00	$100
5790	16" Lighted Christmas Tree	$10.00	$175
6000	6" Candy Box	$2.00	$40
6001	6" Cookie Dish	$0.75	$15
6002	2" Candle Holder w/ Red Candle, Pair	$1.35	$27
6003	3 1/2" Christmas Bell	$0.50	$10
6004	Reindeer, 2 Assorted Shaped	$0.80	$16
6005	8" Sleigh Planter/Centerpiece	$2.00	$40
6006	7" Leaf Shape Ashtray	$0.80	$16
6007	12" Relish Dish	$1.35	$27
6008	9 1/2" Two Compartment Dish	$1.50	$30
6009	9 1/2" Three Compartment Dish	$2.25	$45
6010	11 1/2" Four Compartment Dish	$3.00	$60
6011	3" Salt & Pepper Shakers	$0.80	$16
6012	Sugar & Creamer	$1.75	$35
6013	Teapot	$2.50	$50

		O.P.	C.B.V.
6014	6" Candy Box	$1.50	$30
6015	Two Tier Tidbit Tray	$3.00	$60
6016	3" Mug	$0.60	$12
6017	Cup & Saucer	$1.00	$20
6018	9" Dinner Plate	$1.25	$25
6019	4" Candleholder w/ Climber	$1.35	$27
6020	10" Sleigh Planter/Centerpiece	$3.25	$65
6021	11 1/2" Tree Shape Serving Dish	$2.00	$40
6022	8" Tree Shape Serving Dish	$1.00	$20
6023	8 1/2" Lamp w/ Candle	$3.25	$65
6024	6" Gift Shaped Candy Box	$1.75	$35
6025	2 1/2" Tree Shape Salt & Pepper, Pair	$0.75	$15
6026	5 3/4" Oil Lamp w/ Glass Chimney	$0.80	$16
6027	5" Leaf Shaped Candleholder, Pair	$0.55	$11
6028	5" Sleigh	$0.65	$15
6029	Large Candleholder w/ Candle, 4 Pc. Set	$4.50	$85
6030	9" Bell Shaped Serving Dish	$1.00	$20
6031	6 1/2" Oil Lamp w/ Glass Chimney	$0.90	$25
6032	4" Pitcher w/ 5" Bowl	$1.50	$30
6033	5 1/4" Pitcher w/ 7 1/4" Bowl	$2.75	$55
6034	5 1/2" Basket w/ Handle	$2.25	$45
6035	3 1/4" Shoe Salt & Pepper, Pair	$0.75	$15
6036	Mini Sugar & Creamer on Tray	$1.75	$35
6037	3 1/4" Shoe Planter	$0.75	$15
6038	4 3/4" Shoe Planter	$1.25	$25
6039	4 3/4" Basket w/ Handle	$1.00	$20
6040	11" Christmas Tree Lamp, Electric (1970)	$5.00	$100
6041	Cookie Jar	$3.00	$60
7072	5" Candleholder, Pair	$2.75	$45

GREEN HOLLY – 1983

		O.P.	C.B.V.
03348	7" Dish	$3.00	$21
03349	3" Mug	$2.25	$15
03350	9 1/2" Two Compartment Dish	$4.00	$28
03351	8" Dish	$3.75	$26
03352	9" Two Tier Tidbit Tray	$10.00	$60
03353	3 1/2" Bell	$1.75	$12
03354	5" Basket	$3.50	$24
03355	3" Salt & Pepper	$3.00	$15
03356	4" Pitcher w/ Bowl	$4.00	$28
03357	5" Candleholder	$3.00	$21
03418	7" Musical Tree "Jingle Bells"	$13.50	$95
03962	9" Bell Shaped Dish	$4.25	$30
03963	7" Teapot	$10.00	$60
03964	4" Sugar & Creamer	$6.50	$38
03965	9" Plate	$5.00	$35
03966	Cup & Saucer	$5.00	$35
03967	8" Sleigh Planter	$10.00	$65
03968	3 1/4" Shoe Planter	$3.00	$21
03969	6" Candy Box	$6.00	$42

GREEN ORCHARD (GREEN PEAR N APPLE) – 1966

		O.P.	C.B.V.
3731	14" Four Compartment Dish	$3.50	$75
3732	12" Two Compartment Dish	$1.50	$33
3733	Canister Set (Square)	$6.50	$125
3734	5 1/2" Instant Coffee w/ Spoon	$0.80	$18
3740	Covered Butter Dish	$1.10	$24
3742	Teapot	$2.00	$55
3744	Sugar & Creamer	$1.25	$28

3745	5 1/2" Jam Jar w/ Spoon	$0.80	$18
3747	3 1/4" Mug	$0.50	$10
3749	Salt & Pepper	$0.60	$10
3756	7" Dish	$0.60	$10
3761	Canister Set (Round)	$6.50	$125
3762	Cookie Jar (Square)	$2.75	$60
3848	6 1/4" Wall Pocket (1966)	$0.80	$18
3849	7 1/8" Wall Pocket (1966)	$0.80	$18
3850	7 1/4" Wall Pocket (1966)	$0.80	$18
3852	7" Wall Pocket (1966)	$0.80	$18
3853	6" Apple Wall Pocket (1966)	$0.80	$18
4316	4 1/2" Flower Cart Planter	$0.80	$18
4328	3 1/2" Compote Shape Planter	$1.10	$25
4329	5" Planter	$1.25	$28
4330	4" Planter	$0.80	$18
4331	8" Vase Planter	$0.80	$18
4332	6" Compote Shape Planter	$1.35	$30
4379	Wall Hanger, Scale Shape	$1.50	$33
4457	11 3/4" Oil Lamp	$2.50	$55
4458	6 1/2" Pitcher	$1.10	$25
4459	8 1/2" Pitcher	$2.00	$44
4513	14" Lox & Bagel Dish	$4.50	$78
4521	Cookie Jar	$2.50	$60
4689	8" Wall Plaques, Pair Pear/Apple	$0.65	$15
4921	9 1/4" Salad Bowl w/ Wooden Handle	$2.25	$50
4949	Salt & Pepper (Square)	$0.70	$15
4957	5 1/2" Instant Coffee Jar w/ Spoon	$0.90	$20
4978	12" Egg Plate w/ Salt & Pepper	$2.00	$44
5181	8" Double Spoon Rest	$0.65	$16
5198	2 Quart Tureen w/ Ladle & Tray	$7.50	$125

GREEN VINTAGE (GREEN HERITAGE FRUIT) – 1971

		O.P.	C.B.V.
1860	7" Nappy Dish (1965-1966)	$0.65	$52
2720	4 1/2" Candy Box (1965-1966)	$1.50	$75
6263	8 1/2" Coffee Pot (1971)	$4.50	$150
6264	Sugar & Creamer (1971-1972)	$3.00	$65
6265	Cup & Saucer (1971)	$1.75	$50
6266	AD Cup & Saucer (1971)	$1.25	$42
6267	7 1/4" Plate (1971)	$1.00	$45
6268	9" Plate (1971-1972)	$1.50	$58
6269	Jam Jar w/ Plate & Spoon (1971-1973)	$2.00	$60
6270	Salt & Pepper (1971-1972)	$0.90	$38
6271	7 1/2" Teapot (1971-1972)	$4.75	$195
6272	6 1/2" Pitcher (1971-1974)	$4.00	$125
6373	6 1/4" Candy Box (1971)	$3.75	$175
6274	7" Tumble-up (1971)	$3.25	$125
6275	8" Snack Set (1971-1973)	$1.75	$48
6276	Hanagata Cup & Saucer (1971-1972)	$1.10	$40
6277	Two Tier Tidbit Tray (1971)	$4.00	$110
6278	4 1/2" Candy Box (1971-1972)	$2.00	$65
6279	6 1/4" Pitcher w/ 9 1/4" Bowl (1971-1973)	$4.50	$225
6280	5 1/4" Pitcher w/ 7 1/4" Bowl (1971-1973)	$3.00	$155
6281	3 1/4" Pitcher w/ 4 1/2" Bowl (1971-1973)	$1.50	$75
6282	6" Bone Dish (1971)	$0.65	$35
6283	Nappy Dish, 3 shapes (1971-1972)	$1.00	$42
6284	9 1/4" Cake Plate (1971)	$2.00	$84

6285	7" Compote (1971)	$1.50	$63
6286	8 3/4" Vase, 3 shapes (1971-1972)	$2.50	$95
6287	5 1/2" Bud Vase, 3 shapes (1971)	$1.00	$42
6288	3 1/2" Pitcher, 3 shapes (1971-1973)	$0.75	$32
6711	2 Cup Teapot (1971)	$2.00	$85

HEAVENLY ROSE (Collector's Name) – 1956

		O.P.	C.B.V.
099	Sugar & Creamer	$1.00	$40
100	8" Tea & Toast	$0.60	$35
103	Cigarette Set	$1.00	$40
105	9 1/4" Plate w/ Handle	$0.80	$60
106	Bone Dish	$0.30	$25
107	6 1/2" Bon Bon	$0.55	$42
108	Salt & Pepper	$0.30	$25
109	7" Compote	$0.60	$55
519	9" Plate	$1.50	$48
606	9" Compote	$1.75	$48
2689	Sugar & Creamer	$2.00	$55
2690	Coffee Pot	$4.00	$125
2758	7 1/2" Plate	$1.50	$35
2758	Cup & Saucer	$1.00	$40
3063	Jam Jar w/ Plate & Spoon	$1.10	$50
20596	Stacking Teapot, Sugar & Creamer	$3.25	$195

HEIRLOOM (HEIRLOOM ELEGANCE) – 1968

		O.P.	C.B.V.
5381	Coffee Pot	$4.00	$140
5382	Sugar & Creamer	$2.50	$85
5383	Cup & Saucer	$1.50	$52
5384	AD Cup & Saucer	$1.25	$44
5385	Snack Set	$1.50	$52
5386	Jam Jar w/ Plate & Spoon	$1.75	$60
5387	7 1/4" Plate	$1.00	$35
5388	9" Plate	$1.50	$52
5389	Salt & Pepper	$0.65	$35
5390	6 1/2" Bone Dish	$0.65	$35
5391	9" Cake Plate	$2.00	$70
5392	6" Nappy Dish, 3 shapes	$1.00	$35
5393	4 1/2" Candy Box	$2.25	$75
5394	Teapot	$4.00	$140
5395	7" Pitcher	$3.50	$125
5522	3 3/4" Pitcher & Bowl	$1.10	$40
5523	6" Pitcher & Bowl	$2.10	$85

HEIRLOOM ROSE – 1959

		O.P.	C.B.V.
1074	Snack Set	$0.65	$48
1075	Three Piece Tea Set	$2.50	$185
1076	Cup & Saucer	$0.55	$40
1376	Snack Set	$0.65	$48
1377	5" Candy Box	$1.10	$80
1378	Cream & Sugar	$0.40	$30
1379	6" Dish w/ Handle	$0.40	$30
1380	8 1/4" Bonbon Dish	$0.60	$45
1381	7 1/2" Cake Plate	$0.45	$34
1441	Cigarette Set w/ Lighter	$1.30	$96
1708	11 1/2" Pitcher w/ Cover	$4.00	$225
1709	5 1/4" Candy Box	$3.00	$125
1710	10 3/4" Bread Tray	$2.00	$112
1795	2 1/2" Cigarette Urn w/ Trays	$0.60	$44
1807	4 Nested Ashtrays	$0.60	$44

1821	10" Plate	$1.10	$80
1822	9" Plate	$0.65	$48
1823	7 1/2" Plate	$0.50	$37
1824	9 1/4" Two Compartment Dish	$1.00	$74
1825	9" Dish	$0.80	$60
1826	Cup & Saucer	$0.55	$40
1827	Ice Cream Set	$0.55	$45
1915	Six Piece Condiment Set	$1.00	$74
1916	3 1/2" Candle Holder, Pair	$1.00	$74
1917	8" Vase	$1.00	$74
1937	Sugar & Creamer	$0.55	$40
1938	Powdered Sugar Shaker	$0.50	$37
1956	Assorted Pin Boxes	$0.30	$23
2320	4 Piece Doll Furniture Set (1960)	$3.00	$225
2538	6 1/2" Nappy Dish, 3 kinds	$0.55	$40
8955	Three Piece Tea Set	$2.50	$185

HEIRLOOM VIOLET – 1959

		O.P.	C.B.V.
1074	Snack Set	$0.65	$48
1075	Three Piece Tea Set	$2.50	$185
1076	Cup & Saucer	$0.55	$40
1376	Snack Set	$0.65	$48
1377	5" Candy Box	$1.10	$80
1378	Cream & Sugar	$0.40	$30
1379	6" Dish w/ Handle	$0.40	$30
1380	8 1/4" Bonbon Dish	$0.60	$45
1381	7 1/2" Cake Plate	$0.45	$34
1441	Cigarette Set w/ Lighter	$1.30	$96
1795	2 1/2" Cigarette Urn w/ Trays	$0.60	$45
1807	4 Nested Ashtrays	$0.60	$45
1956	Assorted Pin Boxes	$0.30	$23
2538	6 1/2" Nappy Dish	$0.55	$40

HOLIDAY GARLAND – 1977

		O.P.	C.B.V.
1052	3 3/4" Footed Mug	$1.35	$13
1053	4" Mug	$1.25	$12
1054	10 1/4" Cake Plate	$7.00	$56
1055	10 1/4" Cake Plate w/ Handle	$4.00	$32
1056	8" Plate	$1.65	$17
1248	8 3/4" Coffee Pot	$7.00	$48
1249	Sugar & Creamer	$5.50	$30
1250	8" Compote	$4.00	$32
1299	Cup & Saucer	$2.25	$18

HOLLY GARLAND (Collector's Name) – 1959

		O.P.	C.B.V.
1402	8" Snack Set	$0.65	$40
1802	Cup & Saucer	$0.55	$35
1803	7 1/2" Plate	$0.50	$32
1804	9" Plate	$0.60	$40
1964	Coffee Pot	$2.00	$125
1965	Cream & Sugar	$1.00	$60
1966	Salt & Pepper	$0.35	$25
2038	3 Compartment Dish	$2.00	$125
2039	Jam Jar w/ Spoon & Under Plate	$1.00	$60
2040	Egg Cup	$0.35	$35
2041	Mug	$0.50	$30
2093	Double Tidbit Tray	$2.00	$95
2094	Single Tidbit Tray	$0.65	$40
2095	Bonbon Dish, 2 kinds	$0.55	$34

HOLLY LEAVES AND BERRIES (Collector's Name) – 1986

		O.P.	C.B.V.
05230	10" Plate	$6.00	$24
05231	8" Plate	$3.00	$12
05232	Cup & Saucer	$4.00	$16
05233	7" Teapot	$12.50	$50
05234	Sugar & Creamer	$7.50	$30
05235	3 3/4" Leaf Shaped Dish	$3.00	$12
05236	5 1/2" Oval Dish	$3.50	$14
05237	5" Round Dish	$2.75	$11
05238	2 1/2" Salt & Pepper	$3.25	$13
05239	4" Napkin Holder	$3.50	$14
05240	3 1/2" Bell	$2.25	$10
05241	4 1/2" Hurricane Lamp w/ Candle	$4.50	$18
05242	6 Napkin Rings	$7.50	$30
05243	4 1/2" Footed Mug	$2.50	$10
05244	4" Mug	$2.50	$10
05245	9" Two Tier Tidbit Tray	$12.50	$48
05246	7 1/2" Tree Shaped Dish	$4.50	$18
05247	6 1/2" Bud Vase, 3 kinds	$3.00	$12
05248	4 1/2" Pitcher w/ Bowl	$3.75	$15
05249	5" Bell	$3.00	$12
05250	3 1/4" Tree Shaped Box	$2.50	$10
05251	3 1/2" Candleholder	$3.25	$13
05252	4 1/2" Candle Holder	$4.00	$16
05253	3" Basket	$2.00	$10
05254	2" Pin Box, 3 kinds	$2.00	$10
05255	AD Cup & Saucer	$3.50	$14
05363	6 3/4" Candelabrum	$5.00	$20
05364	5" Candelabrum	$3.25	$15
05365	7" Advent Wreath	$10.00	$40
05366	6 1/2" Advent Wreath	$7.50	$30
05847	3 1/2" Mug	$2.50	$10

HOLLY WITH TOUCHES OF CANDY CANE RED (Collector's Name) – 1957

		O.P.	C.B.V.
025	9" Plate	$0.60	$30
026	Cup & Saucer	$0.55	$25
027	11" 3 Compartment Relish Tray	$1.25	$56
028	8 1/2" Three Section Serving Plate	$1.50	$67
029	Cream & Sugar	$1.00	$45
030	Cigarette Box w/ 2 Ash Trays	$1.00	$45
031	Two Section Serving Plate	$1.00	$45
032	3 Piece Console Set	$2.50	$95
033	Candle Holder, Pair	$1.25	$48
034	Salt & Pepper	$0.55	$25
035	Jam Jar w/ Spoon, Tray, Salt & Pepper	$1.00	$65
036	7 1/2" Compote	$1.25	$55
037	Cookie Jar	$2.00	$125
038	Candy Box	$1.00	$45
039	Jam Jar w/ Spoon & Under Plate	$0.80	$36
116	Single Tidbit Tray	$0.90	$40
210	10" Punch Bowl & 8 Mugs	$5.40	$225
211	Mugs	$0.40	$18
214	8" Snack Set	$0.80	$36
647	10" Plate	$0.90	$40
725	Cookie Jar	$2.00	$125
735	Cake Plate & Serving Knife	$2.50	$85
736	14" 3 Compartment Relish Tray	$2.00	$90
738	Two Tier Tidbit Tray	$2.00	$75
739	Gravy Boat w/ Under Plate	$1.25	$55
741	Tumbler	$0.40	$35
742	6 Cup Teapot	$1.50	$135
1292	15" Leaf Shaped Celery Dish	$1.25	$55
1293	7" Leaf Shaped Nappy Dish	$0.30	$30
1294	8" Christmas Tree Shaped Nappy Dish	$0.80	$36
1586	Double Dip w/ Ladle	$1.00	$45
2146	5" Pitcher	$0.80	$55

HONEY BEE (Bee Line Label) – 1960

		O.P.	C.B.V.
1278	Tea Pot	$1.50	$110
1279	Cookie Jar	$2.00	$135
1280	Jam Jar w/ Cover	$0.80	$40
1281	Milk Mug	$0.50	$40
1284	Egg Cup	$0.30	$25
1285	Cheese Dish w/ Cover	$1.00	$45
1286	Three Compartment Dish	$1.50	$48
1287	Two Compartment Dish	$1.00	$40
1288	Salt & Pepper Shakers	$0.50	$28
1289	Spoon Rest w/ Shaker	$0.60	$30
1290	Butter Dish w/ Cover	$0.75	$36
1291	Sugar & Creamer	$1.00	$55
1527	Wall Pocket	$0.00	$65
1588	5" Double Jam Dish w/ Spoon	$1.00	$25
1591	12 1/2" Celery Dish	$0.00	$48

HOT POPPY – 1968

		O.P.	C.B.V.
4597	4" Basket	$1.00	$15
5308	Canister Set	$9.00	$135
5398	8 1/2" Pitcher	$3.00	$45
5399	Cookie Jar	$4.00	$60
5400	6 1/2" Salt & Pepper	$1.75	$25
5401	7" Pitcher	$1.50	$23
5405	Jam Jar w/ Spoon	$1.10	$16
5843	5 1/2" Napkin Holder	$1.50	$22
5844	8" Double Spoon Rest	$1.00	$15
5845	12" Two Compartment Dish	$2.50	$37
4846	2 Quart Tureen w/ Ladle & Tray	$10.00	$95
5847	12" Egg Plate w/ Salt & Pepper	$2.75	$40
5963	Covered Butter Dish	$1.50	$25

LILAC CHINTZ – 1963

		O.P.	C.B.V.
129	Teabag Holder	$0.30	$35
130	Compote	$0.75	$65
131	5 1/2" Candy Box	$1.50	$95
202	Jam Jar w/ Tray & Spoon	$1.10	$75
208	Sugar & Creamer w/ Tray	$1.10	$75
700	Salt & Pepper	$0.40	$35
692	Nested Ashtrays	$0.65	$55
693	Teapot	$2.00	$175
694	Sugar & Creamer	$1.10	$75
695	Cup & Saucer	$0.60	$48
696	Cup & Saucer	$0.45	$40
697	Snack Set	$0.90	$50
698	Egg Cup	$0.35	$45
699	6 1/4" Bone Dish	$0.40	$35
701	7 1/4" Plate	$0.50	$45

702	9 1/4" Plate	$0.75	$65
1004	3 1/3" Shell Shaped Teabag Holder or Ashtray	$0.25	$32
1005	5 1/4" Ashtray/Cigarette Holder	$0.50	$45
1279	Two Tier Tidbit Tray	$2.10	$125
1344	3" Cigarette Urn w/ 2 Trays	$0.65	$45

MAGNOLIA – 1961

		O.P.	C.B.V.
2518	Coffee Pot	$1.50	$87
2519	Teapot	$1.50	$87
2520	Sugar & Creamer	$1.00	$45
2521	9" Plate	$0.65	$37
2522	7 1/2" Plate	$0.45	$28
2523	Cup & Saucer	$0.60	$35
2524	AD Cup & Saucer	$0.45	$28
2599	8" Snack Set	$0.65	$35
2618	6" Lemon Plate	$0.45	$26
2623	6 1/2" Bone Dish	$0.35	$20
2639	Salt & Pepper	$0.50	$30

MASONIC – 1955

		O.P.	C.B.V.
2342	Cup & Saucer	$1.00	$15
2343	8" Plate	$1.00	$15
4345	4" Ash Tray	$0.50	$8
6346	8" Lattice Edge Plate	$1.50	$22
20202	5 1/2" Teapot	$1.00	$15

MIDNIGHT ROSE – 1990

		O.P.	C.B.V.
07389	6" Bud Vase	$7.00	$14
07393	5" Bud Vase	$5.50	$11
07394	4 1/2" Pillow Vase	$7.00	$14
07399	10" Vase	$20.00	$40
07401	8" Vase	$11.00	$22
07402	8" Temple Jar	$20.00	$40
07403	6" Temple Jar	$12.50	$25
07431	10" Temple Jar	$27.50	$55
07432	5 3/4" Ginger Jar	$14.00	$28
07433	5" Ginger Jar	$12.00	$24
07483	10 1/4" Plate	$12.00	$24
07384	8 1/4" Plate	$7.50	$15
07385	6 1/4" Book	$4.50	$10
07386	10" Vase	$20.00	$40
07387	8" Vase	$15.00	$30
07388	6" Vase	$10.00	$20
07390	5" Frame	$6.50	$13
07391	3" Box	$5.00	$10
07392	3 3/4" Box	$6.50	$13
07395	5" Bell	$6.00	$12
07396	AD Cup & Saucer	$4.50	$15
07497	7" Frame	$13.00	$26
07398	3 1/2" Candleholder	$7.50	$15

MISS PRISS – 1960

		O.P.	C.B.V.
1502	Cookie Jar	$1.50	$185
1503	4" Mug	$0.50	$75
1504	Pitcher	$0.75	$155
1505	Cheese Dish w/ Cover	$0.80	$275
1506	Tea Bag Holder	$0.25	$55
1507	Two Compartment Dish	$1.00	$185
1508	Sugar & Creamer	$1.00	$65

1509	Wall Pocket	$0.55	$150
1510	Egg Cup	$0.25	$65
1511	Salt & Pepper	$0.50	$39
1515	Jam Jar	$0.75	$110
1516-4	4 Cup Teapot	$1.25	$125
1516-6	6 Cup Teapot	$1.50	$150
1524	Ash Tray	$0.55	$60
1525	Spoon Rest w/ Shaker	$0.75	$225
3553	Baby Set, 5" Mug & 6" Bowl	$1.25	$150
3860	5 1/2" Planter	$1.10	$85
4916	6 1/2" Bank (1968)	$2.25	$200

MISTY ROSE – 1969

		O.P.	C.B.V.
5517	Candy Dish, 3 shapes	$1.00	$25
5518	Salt & Pepper	$0.75	$25
5519	7 1/4" Plate	$0.80	$25
5520	9" Plate	$1.25	$35
5521	3 Legged Cup & Saucer	$1.50	$40
5536	Coffee Pot	$4.50	$150
5537	Sugar & Creamer	$2.25	$50
5538	4 3/4" Candy Box	$2.50	$65
5539	Jam Jar w/ Plate & Spoon	$1.50	$40
5690	Snack Set	$1.50	$40
5691	Teapot	$4.50	$125
5692	7" Pitcher	$4.00	$100
5693	5" Candy Box	$2.25	$60
5694	6 1/4" Pitcher & 5" Bowl	$2.75	$75
5695	Bud Vase, 3 kinds	$0.90	$25
5696	5" Compote	$1.50	$40
5697	8" Carafe (Tumble-Up)	$3.50	$95
5698	9 1/4" Cake Plate w/ Handle	$2.00	$50
5699	9" Two Tier Tidbit	$4.00	$100
5700	Tumbler & Soap Dish	$4.00	$100
5724	6 1/2" Leaf Shape Nappy	$0.80	$28
5725	3 1/2" Pitcher w/ 5" Bowl	$1.25	$33
5726	5 1/4" Pitcher w/ 7" Bowl	$2.25	$60
5727	6 1/4" Pitcher w/ 9" Bowl	$4.00	$100
5733	10 1/4" Silent Butler	$4.00	$100
5759	7 3/4" Nappy Dish	$1.00	$27
6130	6 1/4" Candy Box	$3.50	$95

MOSS ROSE (Collector's Name) – 1963

		O.P.	C.B.V.
705	Cup & Saucer	$0.45	$18
706	6" Bone Dish	$0.50	$20
710	Jam Jar w/ Plate & Spoon	$0.80	$32
922	Salt & Pepper	$0.40	$16
1618	17 Piece Starter Set (1964)	$5.40	$215
3166	Coffee Pot	$2.00	$80
3167	Sugar & Creamer	$1.10	$44
3168	9" Plate	$0.60	$24
3169	8" Plate	$0.50	$20
3170	Cup & Saucer	$0.60	$24
3171	Snack Set	$0.65	$26

MOSS VIOLET (Collector's Name) – 1964

		O.P.	C.B.V.
1618	17 Piece Starter Set	$5.40	$215

MR. TOODLES – 1962

		O.P.	C.B.V.
1682	5 1/2" Bank	$0.60	$110
2631	5 1/2" Planters, (2 Poses, 2 Colors)	$0.80	$125

3235	Salt & Pepper	$0.60	$45
3236	Cookie Jar	$2.05	$175
3290	Jam Jar w/ Spoon	$0.75	$55
3291	Teapot	$2.50	$175
3292	Sugar & Creamer	$1.00	$75
3293	Childs Set 6" bowl, 4" Mug	$1.25	$95
3294	6 3/4" Butter Dish	$0.80	$60
3295	Egg Cup	$0.30	$30
3673	Baby Set, 4" Mug & 6" Bowl	$1.25	$95
3974	Salt & Pepper, Pink & Blue Bow, (1966)	$0.65	$45
3975	Sugar & Creamer, Pink & Blue Bow (1966)	$1.25	$75
3976	5" Jam Jar w/ Spoon (1966)	$0.80	$55
4021	Cookie Jar $2.50 (1966)	$2.25	$155
4022	Teapot, Pink Bow (1966)	$1.50	$150

MUSHROOM FOREST – 1971

		O.P.	C.B.V.
6352	Cookie Jar	$4.00	$60
6353	Canister Set	$10.00	$110
6354	12" Egg Tray w/ Salt & Pepper	$3.00	$45
6355	6 1/2" Salt & Pepper	$1.75	$25
6356	4" Mug	$0.90	$13
6357	8" Double Spoon Rest	$1.00	$15
6358	5 1/4" Jam Jar w/ Spoon	$1.25	$20
6359	12" Two Compartment Dish	$2.50	$38
6360	5" Napkin Holder	$1.50	$23
6361	9" Plate	$1.35	$20
6464	2 Quart Soup Tureen w/ Tray & Ladle	$10.00	$150
6465	7" Gravy Boat w/ Tray	$1.75	$26
6466	6 3/4" Pitcher	$1.50	$23
6467	6" Sprinkler Planter	$2.25	$33
6468	7 1/2" Covered Butter Dish	$1.75	$28
6469	5 1/2" Pitcher w/ 6 1/2" Bowl	$3.00	$45
6470	6 1/2" Cart Planter	$1.50	$23
6471	6" Compote Planter	$1.50	$23
6472	6 1/2" Urn Planter	$2.00	$30
6473	5" Basket Planter	$1.25	$18
6474	12" Hors d'oeuvre Dish	$5.00	$65
6524	9" Cart Planter	$2.75	$40

ORDER OF EASTERN STAR – 1955

		O.P.	C.B.V.
100	Teapot	$1.75	$40
102	Sugar & Creamer	$1.10	$24
103	Salt & Pepper Shakers	$0.60	$13
104	9" Plate	$0.60	$14
105	7" Plate	$0.45	$10
106	Snack Set	$0.65	$15
107	Cup & Saucer	$0.60	$14
108	Cup & Saucer	$0.45	$10
111	Coffee Pot	$1.75	$40
559	6 3/4" Ashtray	$0.25	$8
907	Snack Set	$0.60	$14
2337	Cup & Saucer	$1.00	$20
2338	8" Plate	$1.00	$20
2514	6 1/2" Nappy Dishes, 3 kinds	$0.60	$14
2725	Teapot	$2.00	$45
2789	Sugar & Creamer	$1.20	$26
3788	Salt & Pepper	$0.30	$10
4340	4 1/2" Ash Tray	$0.50	$11

4379	Wall Hanging, Scale Shape	$1.50	$33
6341	8" Lattice Edge Plate	$1.50	$33

PAISLEY FANTAZIA (NEW PAISLEY) – 1971

		O.P.	C.B.V.
6793	8 1/2" Coffee Pot	$3.00	$75
6794	5" Sugar & Creamer	$1.75	$45
6795	6 1/2" Teapot	$3.00	$75
6796	5" Sugar & Creamer	$1.75	$40
6797	Two Cup Teapot	$1.00	$45
6798	5" Jam Jar w/ Plate & Spoon	$1.50	$38
6799	9 1/2" Two Tier Tidbit Tray	$4.00	$95
6800	Cup & Saucer	$1.25	$30
6801	Cup & Saucer	$0.80	$20
6802	AD Cup & Saucer	$0.90	$23
6803	7 1/4" Plate	$0.90	$23
6804	9" Plate	$1.40	$35
6805	Compote	$1.25	$32
6806	3 1/2" Pitcher w/ Bowl	$1.25	$32
6807	5 1/2" Pitcher w/ Bowl	$2.50	$62
6808	6" Pitcher w/ Bowl	$4.00	$95
6809	4 1/2" Candy Box	$1.75	$45
6810	6 1/2" Vase, 3 shapes	$0.80	$20
6811	5 1/2" Pitcher Vase, 3 shapes	$0.80	$20
6812	Nested Ashtrays	$1.25	$32
6813	2 1/2" Sugar & Creamer	$1.00	$25
6814	5 1/4" Bell	$0.80	$20
6815	4 1/2" Teabag Holder	$0.40	$14
6931	17 Piece Coffee Set	$7.50	$185

PEAR N APPLE (MUSTARD) – 1966

		O.P.	C.B.V.
3739	Covered Butter Dish	$1.10	$28
3741	Teapot	$2.00	$50
3743	Sugar & Creamer	$1.25	$31
3746	3" Mug	$0.50	$12
3748	Salt & Pepper	$0.60	$15
3755	Canister Set	$6.00	$110
3766	7" Candy Box	$1.75	$43
3848	6 1/4" Wall Pocket	$0.80	$20
3849	7 1/8" Wall Pocket	$0.80	$20
3850	7 1/4" Wall Pocket	$0.80	$20
3851	6" Pear Wall Pocket	$0.80	$20
3852	7" Wall Pocket	$0.80	$20
3853	6" Apple Wall Pocket	$0.80	$20
4127	5" Jam Jar w/ Spoon	$0.80	$20
4128	14" x 12" Four Compartment Dish	$3.50	$85
4129	12" Two Compartment Dish	$1.50	$38
4130	Cookie Jar (Square)	$2.75	$68
4131	Canister Set	$6.00	$110
4132	7 1/2" Plate	$0.60	$15
4133	5 1/2" Instant Coffee Jar	$0.80	$20
4333	6 1/2" Pitcher	$1.10	$28
4334	9" Pitcher	$2.00	$50
4335	Cookie Jar (Round)	$2.50	$65
4336	11 3/4" Oil Lamp	$2.50	$63
4514	14" Lox & Bagel Dish	$4.50	$85
4689	8" Wall Plaques, Pair Pear/Apple	$0.65	$15
4918	12" Egg Plate w/ Salt & Pepper	$2.00	$50
4920	9 1/4" Salad Bowl w/ Wooden Handle	$2.25	$57
4948	Salt & Pepper (Square)	$0.70	$18
4956	5 1/2" Instant Coffee Jar w/ Spoon	$0.90	$23

No.	Item	O.P.	C.B.V.
4977	12" Egg Plate w/ Salt & Pepper	$2.00	$50
5180	8" Double Spoon Rest	$0.65	$16
5197	2 Quart Tureen w/ Ladle & Tray	$7.50	$145

PEAR AND APPLE (Collector's Name) – 1966

No.	Item	O.P.	C.B.V.
4252	Coffee Pot	$2.50	$90
4253	Sugar & Creamer	$1.25	$45
4254	Cup & Saucer	$0.90	$33
4255	Jam Jar w/ Plate & Spoon	$1.25	$45
4256	7" Plate	$0.55	$20
4257	9" Plate	$0.75	$27
4258	Teapot	$2.50	$105
4259	Salt & Pepper	$0.45	$15
4260	6 1/2" Pitcher	$1.50	$55
4261	AD Cup & Saucer	$0.75	$27
4262	6 1/2" Bone Dish	$0.45	$18
4263	Tea & Toast	$0.90	$33
4316	4 1/2" Flower Cart	$0.80	$30
4328	3 1/2" Compote Shape Planter	$1.10	$40
4329	5" Planter	$1.25	$45
4330	4" Planter	$0.80	$29
4331	8" Vase	$0.80	$45
4332	6" Compote Shaped Planter	$1.35	$48

PETITES FLEURS – 1971

No.	Item	O.P.	C.B.V.
6433	2 Piece Bathroom Set	$1.75	$38
6434	5 1/8" Lipstick Holder	$0.80	$18
6435	4" Toothbrush Holder	$0.80	$18
6436	4 3/4" Toothpick Holder	$0.60	$14
6437	2 1/4" Salt & Pepper w/ Handle	$1.10	$24
6839	5" Double Switch Plate	$0.85	$18
6840	5 1/4" Single Switch Plate	$0.65	$15
6841	2 Cup Teapot	$2.00	$44
6842	Sugar & Creamer	$1.35	$30
6843	3 1/4" Pitcher w/ 4 1/2" Bowl	$1.10	$24
7050	6" Two Compartment Dish	$0.60	$18
7051	Sugar & Creamer w/ Tray	$1.50	$33
7052	7" Nappy Dish, 3 kinds	$1.35	$30
7053	7" Bud Vase, 3 kinds	$0.90	$20
7054	3 1/2" Bell	$0.60	$14
7055	Covered Box, 2 shapes	$0.60	$14
7056	8" Three Compartment Dish	$2.00	$44

PINE CONE – 1961

No.	Item	O.P.	C.B.V.
350	5 1/4" Candleholder, Pair	$1.00	$40
351	Salt & Pepper Shakers	$0.40	$16
352	9" Two Compartment Dish	$0.80	$32
353	6" Teapot	$1.10	$45
355	Sugar & Creamer	$1.00	$40
2460	6 1/4" Vase, 3 kinds	$1.00	$40
2461	6" Pitcher Vase, Left & Right	$1.10	$44
2466	3 1/2" Ashtray	$0.35	$14
2477	4" Wall Plaque	$0.55	$22
2478	6 1/2" Wall Plaque	$1.10	$44
2479	4" Vase, 3 kinds	$0.55	$22
2480	2 1/4" Mini Vase, 3 kinds	$0.30	$12
2481	3" Bell	$0.50	$20
20118	Snack Set (1956)	$1.10	$44

PINK CLOVER – 1961

No.	Item	O.P.	C.B.V.
2483	16 Piece Starter Set	$6.00	$270
2484	Cup & Saucer	$0.55	$25
2485	6 Cup Teapot	$1.75	$80
2486	Sugar & Creamer	$1.05	$48
2487	5 1/2" Pitcher	$0.80	$36
2488	4 1/4" Jam Jar w/ Spoon	$0.80	$36
2489	7" Butter Dish w/ Cover	$0.80	$36
2490	6 1/2" Cheese Dish w/ Cover	$1.00	$45
2491	10 1/2" Two Compartment Dish	$1.05	$48
2492	9" Three Compartment Dish	$1.55	$70
2493	Egg Cup	$0.33	$15
2494	14" Platter	$2.00	$90
2495	10 1/4" Plate	$0.90	$40
2496	6 1/2" Bread & Butter Plate	$0.35	$16
2497	Salt Box	$1.10	$50
2498	7 1/4" Cookie Jar	$2.00	$90
2499	5" Candy Box	$1.05	$48
2500	Divided Vegetable Bowl	$1.50	$68
2501	9 1/2" Covered Vegetable Bowl	$2.00	$90
2502	7 1/2" Plate	$0.55	$25
2503	6 1/4" Bowl	$0.55	$25
2504	7 1/4" Soup Bowl	$0.55	$25
2505	8 1/2" Gravy Boat w/ Under Plate	$1.25	$56
2506	Two Tier Tidbit Tray	$1.80	$75
2507	9 1/4" Plate	$0.60	$28
2508	9 1/4" Plate w/ Handle	$0.80	$36
2536	Salt & Pepper	$0.55	$25
2601	10 1/2" Salad Bowl	$1.75	$78
2602	11 1/2" Salad Spoon & Fork	$0.50	$22
2603	Snack Set	$0.80	$36
2604	3 1/4" Mug	$0.55	$25
2605	12 1/4" Chop Plate	$1.50	$68
2606	8" Oil & Vinegar Set	$1.25	$56

PINK DAISY – 1968

No.	Item	O.P.	C.B.V.
5028	6" Planter	$1.75	$26
5029	7" Cart Planter	$2.25	$34
5030	5 1/2" Jardiniere	$1.35	$20
5031	4 1/4" Footed Urn Planter	$1.20	$18
5032	8" Vase	$1.00	$15
5033	5" Instant Coffee Jar w/ Spoon	$2.25	$34
5034	6 1/2" Salt & Pepper	$1.10	$16
5161	14" Chip n Dip Plate	$5.00	$75
5162	8" Spoon Rest	$1.25	$20
5163	3 1/2" Salt & Pepper	$0.64	$12
5164	4" Jam Jar w/ Spoon	$0.90	$18
5165	9 1/2" Three Compartment Bowl w/ Wooden Handle	$2.25	$34
5166	4 1/4" Ivy Pot	$1.00	$15
5167	6 1/2" Footed Planter	$1.75	$26
5190	Sugar & Creamer	$1.35	$20
5191	5 Cup Teapot	$2.25	$34
5192	Cookie Jar	$2.75	$42
5195	Canister Set	$6.50	$98

PINK DOGWOOD – 1990

No.	Item	O.P.	C.B.V.
07237	5 1/2" Bud Vase, 3 kinds,	$6.00	$18

		O.P.	C.B.V.
07238	8 3/4" Vase, 3 kinds	$17.50	$53
07239	6" Candleholder	$9.00	$27
07241	8 3/4" Coffee Pot	$25.00	$75
07242	4 1/2" Sugar & Creamer	$20.00	$60
07243	Cup & Saucer	$10.00	$30
07244	AD Cup & Saucer	$7.50	$22
07245	Teapot	$25.00	$75
07246	Cup & Saucer	$9.00	$27
07247	9" Plate	$9.00	$27
07248	7 1/4" Plate	$6.00	$18
07249	9" Cake Plate	$12.00	$36
07250	5 1/2" Tumble-up	$16.50	$50
07252	4 1/4" Pitcher w/ Bowl	$17.50	$53
07253	2 3/8" Salt & Pepper	$7.00	$21
07254	Nappy Dish, 3 kinds	$6.00	$18

POINSETTIA (Limited Edition) – 1967

		O.P.	C.B.V.
4383	Teapot	$3.25	$110
4384	Sugar & Creamer	$2.00	$68
4385	Jam Jar w/ Plate & Spoon	$1.25	$42
4386	AD Cup & Saucer	$0.90	$30
4387	Candy Box	$1.75	$60
4388	Teapot	$3.25	$110
4389	6 1/4" Pitcher	$3.00	$90
4390	Salt & Pepper	$0.50	$22
4391	Two Tier Tidbit Tray	$3.25	$85
4392	Cup & Saucer	$1.10	$37
4394	7" Nappy Dish, 3 kinds	$0.75	$25
4395	7 1/4" Plate	$0.65	$28
4396	9" Plate	$1.10	$38
4397	Snack Set	$1.10	$38
4398	6" Bone Dish	$0.80	$25

POINSETTIA – 1988

		O.P.	C.B.V.
04631	10" Plate	$6.50	$32
06432	8" Plate	$3.75	$19
06433	Cup & Saucer	$6.00	$30
06434	7 1/2" Tree Shaped Dish	$5.00	$25
06435	6 3/4" Leaf Shaped Dish	$3.00	$15
06436	5 1/2" Oval Dish	$4.00	$20
06437	5" Round Dish	$3.50	$18
06438	2 3/4" Salt & Pepper	$4.00	$20
06439	5" Bell	$3.75	$19
06440	3 1/2" Candleholder	$3.50	$18
06441	4 1/2" Candleholder	$1.85	$10
06442	3 1/2" Mug	$3.25	$15
06443	7" Teapot	$14.00	$70
06444	Sugar & Creamer	$10.00	$50
06516	7" Bud Vase, 3 kinds	$3.00	$15
06517	4 3/4" Basket	$3.00	$15
06518	2 1/4" Pin Box	$2.75	$14
06642	6 1/2" Leaf Shape Dish	$5.50	$27
06643	6 1/2" Flower Shape Dish	$5.50	$27
06644	6 1/2" Teardrop Shape Dish	$5.50	$27
06807	3 3/4" Mug	$3.25	$15

ROSE CHINTZ – 1958

		O.P.	C.B.V.
564	5" Teabag Strainer	$0.65	$95
566	Pin Boxes, 3 shapes	$0.45	$28
627	8" Bone Dish	$0.30	$25
637	8" Snack Set	$0.60	$35
649	Two Tier Tidbit Tray	$2.00	$85
650	7" Compote	$0.60	$55
651	Single Tidbit Tray	$0.60	$35
654	Urn Cigarette Holder w/ 2 Trays	$0.55	$40
656	Cup & Saucer	$0.55	$40
658	7 1/2" Plate	$0.45	$28
659	9" Meat Plate	$0.65	$40
660	8 3/4" Coffee Pot	$2.00	$145
661	Sugar & Creamer	$1.00	$65
662	Cup & Saucer	$0.55	$45
663	Sugar & Creamer	$0.55	$45
664	Egg Cup	$0.30	$55
665	2 3/4" Salt & Pepper	$0.30	$28
666	Square Set of Nesting Ashtrays	$0.55	$35
679	6 1/4" Bud Vases, 3 kinds	$0.55	$45
683	5" Ashtray	$0.30	$28
686	5 1/2" Kerosene Lamp	$0.50	$30
788	Cigarette Box w/ 2 Trays	$0.65	$40
793	6 1/2" Bone Dish	$0.30	$22
794	Sugar & Creamer, 2 kinds	$0.50	$32
890	5 1/2" Jar w/ Corked Lid	$0.55	$65
891	Jam Jar w/ Spoon & Plate	$0.55	$65
911	6 1/2" Teapot	$1.38	$165
912	Sugar & Creamer	$0.75	$65
1239	Pin Boxes, 3 kinds	$1.00	$25
1512	Cup & Saucer	$0.35	$28
1793	Tea Bag Holder	$0.30	$75
1979	Mug & Saucer	$0.35	$48
2044	3 1/4" Sugar & Creamer w/ Tray	$1.00	$48
2107	10" Cake plate w/ Handle	$1.00	$48
2242	Round Set of Nesting Ashtrays	$0.60	$35
2282	10 1/4" Chip & Dip	$1.50	$150
2283	13" Double Dish on Stand	$1.25	$125
2356	Jumbo Cup & Saucer	$0.75	$35
2425	"Happy Anniversary" Cup & Saucer	$0.60	$28
2537	6 1/2" Nappy Dish, 3 kinds	$0.60	$35
2582	Nesting Ashtrays	$0.55	$35
2744	Covered Butter Dish	$0.75	$75
3064	Jam Jar w/ Plate & Spoon	$1.15	$48
3185	2 Cup Teapot	$0.55	$55
3354	6" Tile w/ Metal Stand	$0.65	$48

ROSE CHINTZ (w/Purple Flowers) – 1973

		O.P.	C.B.V.
7236	Teapot	$3.25	$55
7237	Sugar & Creamer	$2.25	$33
7238	Cup & Saucer	$1.25	$18
7239	7 1/4" Plate	$1.00	$15
7240	9" Plate	$1.50	$23
7241	Two Tier Tidbit Tray	$4.50	$65
7242	7" Latticed Compote	$1.50	$23
7243	2 Cup Teapot	$1.10	$32
7244	Pitcher & Bowl	$1.50	$23
7245	Sugar & Creamer, 2 kinds	$1.25	$18
7246	5 1/2" Bud Vase, 3 kinds	$0.80	$12
7247	4 1/2" Tea Bag Holder	$0.50	$10
7248	Pin Boxes, 3 kinds	$0.55	$10
7543	9 1/4" Musical Teapot "Tea For Two"	$5.50	$65

ROSE GARDEN – 1971

		O.P.	C.B.V.
7570	8 1/2" Coffee Pot	$4.50	$110

6571	Sugar & Creamer	$3.00	$55
6572	Cup & Saucer	$1.75	$35
6573	AD Cup & Saucer	$1.25	$22
6576	8" Snack Set	$1.75	$35
6577	7" Nappy Dish, 3 shapes	$1.00	$25
6578	Jam Jar w/ Plate & Spoon	$2.00	$38
6579	2 1/2" Salt & Pepper	$0.90	$27
6580	7" Tumble-up	$3.25	$75
6581	4 1/2" Candy Box	$2.25	$48
6582	6 1/2" Bone Dish	$0.65	$20
6583	9 1/4" Cake Plate	$2.00	$48
6584	7 1/2" Teapot	$4.75	$108
6585	6 3/4" Pitcher	$4.00	$78
6586	7" Compote	$1.50	$42
6587	9" Two Tier Tidbit Tray	$4.00	$75
6588	8 1/2" Vase, 3 kinds	$2.50	$65
6589	5" Pitcher Vase, 3 kinds	$1.00	$25
6590	3 1/2" Pitcher, 3 kinds	$0.75	$22
6627	6" Pitcher w/ Bowl	$4.50	$95
6628	5 1/4" Pitcher w/ Bowl	$3.00	$80
6629	3 1/2" Pitcher w/ Bowl	$1.50	$36
6630	6 1/4" Candy Box	$3.75	$95
6632	Cup & Saucer	$1.25	$35
6712	2 Cup Teapot	$2.00	$48
6955	4" Hinged Box, 4 shapes, 2 Colors	$2.25	$55
6956	9 1/2" Silent Butler, 2 Colors	$5.50	$115
6957	5" Hinged Box, 2 colors	$4.00	$75
6958	6" Piano Hinged Box, 2 colors	$4.00	$75
7543	9 1/2" Musical Teapot "Tea For Two"	$5.50	$65

RUSTIC DAISY – 1966

		O.P.	C.B.V.
3855	Teapot	$2.00	$55
3856	Sugar & Creamer	$1.25	$30
3857	Salt & Pepper	$0.65	$16
3858	Jam Jar w/ Spoon	$0.80	$20
3859	Cookie Jar	$2.50	$63
4114	14" x 12" Four Compartment Dish	$3.50	$85
4115	Canister Set	$6.00	$125
4116	5 3/4" Instant Coffee Jar	$0.80	$20
4117	Cup & Saucer	$0.65	$16
4118	7 1/2" Plate	$0.65	$16
4119	9 1/2" Plate	$1.00	$25
4120	Two Tier Tidbit Tray	$2.25	$55
4121	11 1/4" x 6" Relish Dish	$1.10	$28
4122	13" x 7" Two Compartment Dish w/ Handle	$2.00	$50
4123	7 1/2" Spoon Rest	$0.45	$15
4124	Salt & Pepper Shakers	$1.00	$25
4125	8 1/2" Pitcher	$2.10	$50
4126	6 3/4" Pitcher	$1.10	$28
4360	8" Wall Pocket, Hat Shape	$1.50	$38
4466	7 3/4" Covered Butter Dish,	$1.50	$38
4467	6 1/4" Wall Pocket, Pitcher & Bowl Shape	$0.80	$20
4468	3 3/4" Mug	$0.55	$13
4483	13" Lavabo, 3 Piece Set	$2.00	$50
5002	6" Compote Shape Planter	$1.10	$28
5003	5" Jardiniere	$1.25	$33
5004	6 1/2" Cart Planter	$2.10	$48
5005	5 3/4" Compote	$1.35	$34
5006	6 3/4" Footed Urn	$1.35	$34
5007	4" Jardiniere	$0.80	$20
5008	8" Flower Vase	$0.90	$23
5182	12" Egg Plate w/ Salt & Pepper	$2.00	$50
5196	2 Quart Tureen w/ Ladle & Tray	$7.50	$155
5402	7" Matchbox Holder	$1.25	$32
5403	6" Napkin Holder	$1.35	$34
5404	8 1/2" Pitcher w/ 6 Glasses & Tray	$7.50	$155
5408	6" Candleholder w/ Candle	$4.00	$48
5564	6 1/2" Cereal Bowl	$0.90	$35
5565	6" Pitcher & Bowl	$2.25	$55
5907	12 Piece Coffee Set	$7.50	$185
5981	5" Egg Candy Box	$1.25	$32

SHAMROCK PORCELAIN – 1981

		O.P.	C.B.V.
00245	4" Basket	$2.50	$15
02522	4" Planter	$3.25	$20
02609	4" Bell	$1.65	$10
02610	5" Bell	$2.25	$14
02612	6 1/2" Vase, 3 kinds	$3.00	$18
02613	6" Dish	$2.50	$15
02614	2" Pin Box, 3 kinds	$1.75	$10
02615	3" Pin Box	$2.00	$12
02616	2 1/2" Pin Box	$2.75	$16
02617	4" Bag Planter	$3.25	$20
02618	5" Picture Frame	$3.50	$21
02635	8" Pen Tray	$2.50	$20
02636	5" Dish	$2.50	$15
02682	5" Footed Mug	$3.00	$18
02683	4" AD Cup & Saucer	$2.50	$15
02684	3 3/4" Footed Mug	$2.50	$15
02836	4 1/2" Bell	$3.75	$22
02910	3" Basket	$2.00	$12
RE2819	Jewel Box	$7.50	$45
03056	23 Piece Starter Set	$42.80	$250
03080	7" Teapot	$10.00	$60
03081	Sugar & Creamer	$6.00	$36
03082	7" Plate	$2.50	$15
03083	Cup & Saucer	$3.75	$23
03084	4 1/2" Pitcher w/ Bowl	$3.25	$20
03085	9" Two Tier Tidbit Tray	$10.00	$60
03086	5 1/2" Frame	$3.75	$23
03290	6" Musical Teapot "Irish Eyes ... "	$12.50	$75
03292	2 1/4" Salt & Pepper	$2.50	$15
03293	9" Plate	$5.00	$30
03314	5" Mug	$3.00	$18
03315	4" Footed Mug	$3.00	$18
03330	6 Napkin Rings	$7.50	$45
03337	3 3/4" Mug	$2.00	$12
03380	3" Candleholder	$2.50	$15
03410	4 1/2" Double Frame	$2.75	$17
03411	3" Frame	$2.00	$12
03412	3 1/2" Heart Shaped Frame	$2.50	$15
03413	4" Oval Frame	$2.50	$15
03414	4" Frame	$2.60	$16
03669	2 1/2" Salt & Pepper	$2.50	$15
03671	1" Thimble "Lucky Shamrock"	$1.50	$10
03672	1" Thimble	$1.50	$10
03731	3 3/4" Bag	$2.25	$14
03834	5 1/4" Pitcher w/ Bowl	$10.00	$60
03835	6 1/2" Bud Vase	$3.00	$18
04070	2 1/2" Ring Holder	$2.50	$15
04071	3" Tea Strainer	$2.50	$15
04357	3 3/4" Mug	$3.00	$18

		O.P.	C.B.V.
04358	3 3/4" Mug, 4 kinds	$3.00	$18
04359	5" Footed Mugs, 4 kinds	$3.25	$20
04385	6 1/2" Bud Vase	$3.00	$18
04953	Irish Coffee Mug	$5.00	$30
05465	9" Tile Trivet, 2 kinds	$1.25	$8
05964	7 1/4" Bud Vase, 3 kinds	$3.50	$21
05965	3" Box	$3.50	$21
05966	2 1/2" Pin Box	$2.75	$17
06633	3 1/2" Irish Footed Mug	$3.50	$21
06712	3 5/8" Footed Mug	$3.00	$18

SILVER WHEAT – 1958

		O.P.	C.B.V.
224	Snack Set	$0.60	$30
225	Demitasse Sugar & Creamer	$0.55	$27
226	Nest of Ashtrays	$0.55	$27
227	Cigarette Urn w/ 2 Trays	$0.50	$25
229	6" Teapot	$1.25	$62
236	6 Cup Teapot	$1.25	$63
1926	Sugar & Creamer	$0.80	$48
1977	Cup & Saucer	$0.35	$15
2153	Snack Set	$0.60	$30
2154	Sugar & Creamer	$0.75	$38
2155	6" Teapot	$1.25	$63
2156	8 1/2" Coffee Pot	$1.75	$87
2157	Cup & Saucer	$0.35	$15
2158	Cup & Saucer	$0.50	$25
2160	7" Coffee Pot	$1.50	$75
2162	7 1/2" Plate	$0.40	$20
2163	9" Plate	$0.60	$30
2213	Sugar & Creamer	$0.80	$48
2237	Teapot	$2.00	$95
2238	Cream & Sugar	$1.00	$50
2568	8" Teapot	$1.75	$87

SIMPLICITY – 1960

		O.P.	C.B.V.
139-MF	Cup & Saucer	$0.60	$18
140-MF	Cup & Saucer	$0.60	$18
141-MF	Cup & Saucer	$0.60	$18
142-MF	7 1/2" Plate	$0.50	$15
1491	9" Tea & Toast	$0.65	$20
1711	7 1/2" Bud Vase	$0.60	$18
1841	Musical Compote	$2.50	$75
1931	10 1/2" Dinner Plate	$1.25	$38
1931	7 1/2" Tea Plate	$0.55	$17
1931	Cream & Sugar	$2.50	$45
1931	6 1/4" Bread & Butter Plate	$0.45	$14
1931	Teapot	$3.25	$85
1931	12" Platter	$2.25	$65
1931	16" Platter	$5.50	$95
1931	7 3/4" Coup Soup	$0.60	$18
1931	5 3/4" Coup Fruit	$0.45	$14
1931	Cup & Saucer	$0.60	$18
1931	10 1/4" Vegetable Bowl	$2.25	$65
1931	Egg Cup	$0.35	$18
1936	5 1/4" Candle Warmer, 2 Pieces	$1.25	$38
1941	9" Bone Plate	$0.60	$18
1978	Cup & Saucer	$0.35	$15

SPRING BOUQUET – 1967

		O.P.	C.B.V.
4580	Coffee Pot	$2.50	$75
4581	Sugar & Creamer	$1.25	$38
4582	Jam Jar w/ Plastic Spoon	$1.25	$38
4583	Teapot	$2.50	$75
4584	6" Pitcher w/ 9 1/4" Bowl	$3.00	$90
4585	5 1/4" Pitcher w/ 7 1/4" Bowl	$2.00	$60
4586	Salt & Pepper	$0.50	$15
4587	Cup & Saucer	$1.10	$33
4588	AD Cup & Saucer	$0.75	$23
4589	7 1/4" Plate	$0.55	$17
4590	9" Plate	$0.75	$23
4591	Nappy Dish, 3 shapes	$0.65	$20
4829	Ribbed Teapot, Sugar & Creamer Set	$2.25	$70

SPRING BOUQUET (w/Butterflies) – 1975

		O.P.	C.B.V.
335	5" Hinged Box	$4.50	$45
393	10 1/2" Silent Butler	$9.50	$95
394	5 1/2" Hinged Box	$5.50	$55
396	4" Hinged Box	$3.50	$35
397	4" Hinged Box	$2.50	$25
398	2 1/4" Pin Box, 3 kinds	$1.50	$15
473	9" Three Compartment Dish	$5.50	$55
474	8 1/2" Two Compartment Dish	$4.00	$40
504	6" Six Sided Candy Box	$5.50	$55
685	8 3/4" Coffee Pot	$7.00	$70
686	4" Sugar & Creamer	$6.50	$65
687	3" Cup & Saucer	$3.00	$30
688	2" AD Cup & Saucer	$2.25	$23
689	5" Cup & Saucer	$2.50	$25
690	8" Snack Set	$3.00	$30
692	7" Plate	$1.50	$15
693	9" Plate	$2.25	$23
694	9" Cake Plate	$3.50	$35
695	8" Compote	$2.50	$25
696	3 1/2" Pitcher & Bowl	$2.25	$23
697	6" Vase, 3 kinds	$1.75	$18
698	5" Candy Box	$3.25	$32
699	2 1/2" Salt & Pepper	$1.75	$18
759	Nappy Dish, 3 kinds	$2.00	$20
8131	11" Lavabo Set, 3 kinds	$11.00	$110
8132	8" Vase, 3 kinds	$2.00	$20
8133	6" Hinged Box	$9.00	$90
8134	4" Hinged Box, 2 kinds	$3.50	$35
8135	5 1/2" Pitcher w/ Bowl	$6.50	$65
8136	6 1/2" Pitcher w/ Bowl	$9.00	$90
8228	4" Hinged Box	$3.50	$35
8230	10" Compote	$8.00	$80

SWEET VIOLETS – 1962

		O.P.	C.B.V.
2838	10 1/4" Dinner Plate	$1.00	$30
2839	6 1/2" Bread & Butter Plate	$0.40	$15
2840	7 1/2" Plate	$0.50	$18
2841	11" Divided Vegetable Dish	$1.75	$58
2842	7 1/4" Coffee Pot	$1.75	$58
2843	4" Sugar & Creamer	$1.25	$38
2844	4" Salt & Pepper	$0.65	$20
2845	5" Jam Jar w/ Spoon	$1.00	$30
2846	8 1/2" Gravy Boat	$1.50	$45
2847	10" Two Compartment Dish	$1.25	$38
2848	9 1/2" Three Compartment Dish	$1.75	$52
2849	9 1/4" Tidbit Tray	$1.10	$33
2850	Two Tier Tidbit Tray	$2.00	$60

2851	3 1/2" Egg Cup	$0.40	$24
2852	5 1/2" Pitcher	$1.00	$38
2853	7 1/2" Cookie Jar	$2.10	$68
2854	7" Butter Dish	$0.90	$35
2855	3 3/4" Mug	$0.45	$13
2864	16 Piece Starter Set	$7.20	$220
2865	Cup & Saucer	$0.65	$23
2866	7 1/4" Soup Dish	$0.65	$32
2867	12" Platter	$1.35	$48
2868	14" Platter	$2.25	$68
2869	8 1/2" Covered Vegetable Dish	$2.50	$75
2870	10" Salad Bowl	$2.00	$60
2872	10" Salad Fork& Spoon	$0.65	$45
2873	12 1/4" Cake Plate w/ Steel Bladed Cutter	$2.75	$80
2874	8 1/2" Snack Set	$1.00	$30
2875	Canister Set	$6.00	$150
2876	5" Spice Jar	$0.65	$28
2877	7" Oil & Vinegar Set	$1.50	$50
2878	5 1/2" Candy Box	$1.25	$38
2879	6" Candleholders, Pair	$1.50	$45
2880	8" Two Compartment Dish	$1.00	$32
2881	2 1/2" Cup & Saucer	$0.50	$18
2882	6" Individual Salad Bowl	$0.60	$20
2890	4 1/2" Ivy Pot	$0.75	$23
2891	6 1/2" Pitcher	$1.35	$48
2892	6 1/2" Covered Cheese Dish	$1.00	$50
2893	7 1/2" Spoon Rest	$0.40	$28
2894	6 1/2" Wall Pocket	$0.65	$38

SYMPHONY IN FRUIT – 1959

		O.P.	C.B.V.
1012	Teapot	$1.00	$30
1013	Sugar & Creamer	$1.50	$45
1014	9" Plate w/ Handle	$0.75	$23
1015	15" Leaf Shaped Plate	$1.50	$45
1016	12" Leaf Shaped Plate	$0.75	$23
1017	9" Three Compartment Plate	$1.00	$30
1018	10 1/2" Two Compartment Plate	$0.75	$23
1019	12" Plate w/ Serving Knife	$1.50	$45
1020	10 1/2" Plate w/ Serving Knife	$1.00	$30
1021	8 1/4" Cookie Jar	$1.50	$45
1022	11 3/4" x 4 1/2" Plate	$0.60	$18
1230	Cup & Saucer	$0.55	$16
1231	7" Plate	$0.50	$15
1232	9" Plate	$0.60	$18
1237	10 1/2" Plate	$0.80	$24
1238	Salt & Pepper Shakers	$0.30	$10

THUMBELINA (HONEY BUN) – 1964

		O.P.	C.B.V.
1692	Cookie Jar	$2.00	$130
1695	Teapot	$1.75	$115
1697	Jam Jar w/ Plate & Spoon	$1.00	$65
1708	Sugar & Creamer	$1.25	$80
1711	Salt & Pepper	$0.60	$35

TISKET A TASKET – 1972

		O.P.	C.B.V.
7065	Canister	$15.00	$110
7128	Cookie Jar	$5.00	$60
7129	6 3/4" Salt & Pepper	$2.25	$25
7130	5 1/4" Pitcher w/ Bowl	$3.50	$45

7131	Sugar & Creamer	$2.50	$28
7132	Teapot	$3.25	$48
7133	3 7/8" Mug	$1.10	$13
7134	2 Quart Soup Tureen w/ Tray & Ladle	$12.50	$125
7297	7 3/4" Covered Butter Dish	$2.25	$28
7298	8" Double Spoon Rest	$1.25	$15
7338	5" Wall Pocket	$1.50	$18
7339	12" Egg Plate	$3.50	$45
7544	5" Pitcher w/ Bowl	$3.00	$36

TO A WILD ROSE – 1964

		O.P.	C.B.V.
2561	Teapot	$3.00	$90
2562	6 1/2" Pitcher	$2.50	$75
2563	Sugar & Creamer	$1.75	$40
2564	Coffee Pot	$3.00	$90
2566	Cup & Saucer	$1.10	$33
2567	Demi Cup & Saucer	$0.90	$27
2573	7 1/2" Plate	$0.60	$18
2578	9 1/4" Plate	$1.10	$33
2579	Jam Jar w/ Plate & Spoon	$1.25	$37
2580	Tea & Toast	$1.00	$30
2581	7 1/2" Candy Box	$3.00	$85
2582	Tumble-Up	$2.50	$75
2584	Salt & Pepper Shaker	$0.45	$16
2592	Two Tier Tidbit	$3.00	$65
2597	9" Plate w/ Handle	$1.25	$38
2598	6 1/2" Bone Dish	$0.45	$18
2602	7 1/4" Candy Dish, 3 shapes	$0.65	$20
2603	5" Nappy Dish, 3 shapes	$0.35	$18

VINEYARD – 1962

		O.P.	C.B.V.
3028	Coffee Pot	$1.75	$65
3029	Sugar & Creamer	$1.10	$38
3030	Candy Box	$1.25	$46
3031	Jam Jar w/ Spoon	$1.10	$40
3032	Salt & Pepper	$0.60	$22
3033	9 1/2" Three Compartment Dish	$1.75	$65
3034	9 3/4" Two Compartment Dish	$1.10	$40
3035	4" Candleholders, Pair	$1.10	$40
3036	6" Pitcher	$1.20	$44
3279	Cookie Jar	$2.10	$75
3280	Compote	$0.65	$28
3281	Mug	$0.40	$15
3282	11" Relish Tray	$1.00	$37
3370	Two Tier Tidbit Tray	$2.00	$65
3371	9 1/4" Plate	$0.80	$28
3372	Cup & Saucer	$0.60	$23

VIOLET CHINTZ – 1958

		O.P.	C.B.V.
565	Teabag Strainer	$0.65	$95
566	Pin Boxes	$0.45	$28
631	8" Bone Dish	$0.30	$25
638	8" Snack Set	$0.60	$35
649	Two Tier Tidbit Tray	$2.00	$85
650	7" Compote	$7.20	$55
651	Single Tidbit Tray	$0.60	$35
654	Cigarette Urn w/ 2 Ashtrays	$0.66	$40
656	Cup & Saucer	$0.55	$40
658	7 1/2" Plate	$0.45	$28

659	9" Meat Plate	$0.65	$40
660	8 3/4" Coffee Pot	$2.00	$145
661	Sugar & Creamer	$1.00	$65
662	Cup & Saucer	$0.55	$45
663	Sugar & Creamer	$0.55	$45
664	Egg Cup	$0.30	$55
665	2 3/4" Salt & Pepper	$0.30	$28
666	Nest of Ashtrays	$0.55	$35
679	6 1/4" Bud Vases, 3 kinds	$0.55	$45
683	5" Ashtray	$0.30	$28
686	5 1/2" Kerosene Lamp	$0.50	$30
788	Cigarette Box w/ 2 Trays	$0.65	$40
793	6 1/2" Bone Dish	$0.30	$22
794	Sugar & Creamer, 2 kinds	$0.50	$32
891	Jam Jar w/ Plate & Spoon	$0.55	$65
911	6 1/2" Teapot	$1.38	$165
912	Sugar & Creamer	$0.75	$65
1239	Pin Boxes, 3 kinds	$1.00	$25
1512	Cup & Saucer	$0.35	$28
1793	Tea Bag Holder	$0.30	$75
1979	Mug & Saucer	$0.35	$48
2044	3 1/4" Sugar & Creamer w/ Tray	$1.00	$48
2242	Nested Ashtrays	$0.60	$35
2282	10 1/4" Chip & Dip	$1.50	$150
2283	13" Double Dish on Stand	$1.25	$125
2356	Jumbo Cup & Saucer	$0.75	$35
2425	"Happy Anniversary" Cup & Saucer	$0.60	$28
2537	6 1/2" Nappy Dish, 3 kinds	$0.60	$35
2582	4 Nesting Ashtrays	$0.60	$35
2744	Butter Dish	$0.75	$75
2754	Stacking Teapot	$1.50	$150
3064	Jam Jar w/ Plate & Spoon	$1.15	$48
3185	2 Cup Teapot	$0.55	$55
3355	6" Tile w/ Metal Stand	$0.65	$48

WHEAT POPPY (RAISED) – 1978

		O.P.	C.B.V.
1227	Canister Set	$27.50	$110
1228	Cookie Jar	$11.00	$60
1453	8 1/4" Coffee Pot	$5.75	$48
1454	4" Sugar & Creamer	$4.50	$25
1455	5 1/4" Salt & Pepper	$2.75	$16
1456	4 1/2" Jam Jar w/ Spoon	$2.50	$15
1457	5" Napkin Holder	$2.50	$15
8256	3 Quart Soup Tureen w/ Tray & Ladle	$30.00	$110

WHITE CHRISTMAS – 1963

		O.P.	C.B.V.
603	Teapot	$2.00	$80
604	Sugar & Creamer	$1.25	$40
605	Jam Jar w/ Plate & Spoon	$1.00	$35
606	Cup & Saucer	$0.60	$22
608	7 1/2" Cake Plate	$0.60	$22
610	9" Plate	$0.80	$28
611	Two Tier Tidbit Tray	$2.00	$65
825	Salt & Pepper Shakers	$0.60	$22
1339	Punch Bowl	$3.00	$105
1340	Snack Set	$1.00	$35
1341	Candleholders	$1.10	$38
1342	Candy Box	$1.25	$40
1368	11" Christmas Tree Dish	$1.35	$47
1386	Cookie Jar	$2.50	$87

1387	Mug	$0.50	$17
1408	Sleigh	$1.25	$44
1827	7" Candleholder w/ Candle	$2.00	$50
2368	8 1/4" Sleigh	$1.10	$38
2782	8 1/2" Gravy Boat	$2.00	$65
2830	11 3/4" Divided Bowl	$2.25	$75
3062	3" Bell	$0.45	$14

WHITE CLASSIC – 1971

		O.P.	C.B.V.
6375	6" Footed Bowl Planter	$1.75	$26
6381	Cookie Jar	$3.50	$52
6382	Canister Set	$8.50	$127
6383	8 1/2" Coffee Pot	$2.00	$45
6384	Sugar & Creamer	$1.35	$20
6475	5 1/2" Footed Candy Box	$1.75	$26
6476	7 1/2" Covered Butter Dish	$1.35	$20
6477	4 3/4" Jam Jar w/ Spoon	$0.90	$18
6478	4" Salt & Pepper	$0.90	$18
6479	12" Egg Plate w/ Salt & Pepper	$2.25	$35
6480	5 1/4" Footed Mug	$0.80	$12
6481	5" Napkin Holder	$1.10	$16
6482	7" Gravy Boat w/ Tray	$1.50	$23
6483	9 1/4" Footed Cake Plate	$2.50	$38
6484	9 1/4" Plate	$1.35	$20
6485	7 1/2" Plate	$0.90	$14
6486	9 1/4" Two Tier Tidbit	$3.00	$45
6487	2 Quart Soup Tureen w/ Tray & Ladle	$9.00	$115
6488	10" Two Compartment Dish	$1.50	$23
6489	13" Relish Tray	$4.00	$60
6490	5 1/2" Pitcher w/ 5 1/2" Bowl	$1.75	$26
6491	7 1/4" Pitcher	$1.75	$26
6526	3" Candlestick	$0.70	$10
6527	6 Piece Condiment Set	$4.00	$60
7016	12" Soup Tureen w/ Tray & Ladle, 4 kinds	$8.50	$100

WHITE HOLLY – 1969

		O.P.	C.B.V.
6050	6" Candy Box	$2.00	$50
6051	6" Cookie Dish	$0.75	$18
6052	5" Leaf Shape Candle Holder, Pair	$1.35	$34
6053	3 1/2" Christmas Bell	$0.50	$12
6054	7 1/2" Cookie Jar	$3.00	$75
6055	8" Sleigh Planter/Centerpiece	$2.10	$48
6056	7" Leaf Shape Ashtray	$0.80	$20
6057	12" Relish Tray	$1.35	$34
6058	9 1/2" Two Compartment Dish	$1.50	$38
6059	9 1/2" Three Compartment Dish	$2.25	$56
6060	11 1/2" Four Compartment Dish	$3.00	$75
6061	3" Salt & Pepper	$0.80	$20
6062	4" Sugar & Creamer	$1.75	$44
6063	7" Teapot	$2.50	$65
6064	6" Candy Box	$1.50	$38
6065	Two Tier Tidbit Tray	$3.00	$75
6066	3" Mug	$0.60	$15
6067	Cup & Saucer	$1.00	$25
6068	9" Dinner Plate	$1.25	$32
6069	5 1/2" Basket w/ Handle	$1.00	$25
6070	10" Sleigh Planter	$3.25	$65
6071	8" Tree Shaped Serving Dish	$2.00	$48
6072	11 1/2" Tree Shape Serving Dish	$1.00	$25

6073	6" Gift Shaped Box	$1.75	$43
6074	9" Bell Shaped Serving Dish	$1.00	$25
6075	4" Pitcher w/ 5" Bowl	$1.50	$38
6076	5 1/4" Pitcher w/ 7 1/4" Bowl	$2.75	$65

YELLOW TULIP/TULIP GARDEN – 1971

		O.P.	C.B.V.
6735	5 1/4" Teapot	$2.75	$55
6736	5" Sugar & Creamer	$2.00	$40
6737	5" Jam Jar w/ Spoon	$1.10	$22
6738	7" Pitcher	$2.50	$50
6739	10" Two Compartment Dish	$1.75	$35
6740	10" Egg Plate	$2.75	$55
6741	2 1/2" Salt & Pepper	$1.00	$20
6742	5" Urn Planter	$1.25	$25
6743	5 3/4" Compote Planter	$1.50	$30
6744	5 1/2" Jardiniere	$2.00	$40
6745	6 1/2" Urn Planter	$2.00	$40
6760	Cookie Jar	$4.00	$80
7057	3 1/4" Mugs	$1.00	$20
7121	9 1/4" Footed Cake Plate	$3.25	$65
7122	Canister Set	$12.00	$120
7123	2 Quart Soup Tureen w/ Tray & Ladle	$13.50	$125

7124	4 1/2" Footed Mug	$1.10	$20
7125	5" Napkin Holder	$2.00	$38
7126	8" Double Spoon Rest	$1.25	$25
7127	7 1/2" Covered Butter Dish	$2.25	$45

YULETIDE HOLLY – 1972

		O.P.	C.B.V.
7802	9" Coffee Pot	$3.75	$60
7803	4 1/4" Sugar & Creamer	$2.75	$40
7804	Cup & Saucer	$1.25	$20
7805	7 1/4" Plate	$1.10	$18
7807	7" Compote	$1.75	$28
7808	6 1/4" Bud Vase, 3 kinds	$0.90	$15
7809	4 1/2" Candy Box	$2.25	$36
7810	6" Pitcher & Bowl	$3.50	$55
7811	3 3/4" Pitcher & Bowl	$1.75	$28
7812	5 1/4" Bell	$1.10	$18
7813	Nappy Dish, 3 kinds	$1.25	$20
7814	9 1/4" Plate	$1.75	$28
7815	6" Plate	$0.75	$14
7816	3 3/4" Mug	$1.10	$18
7820	4 1/2" Candleholder	$1.10	$18
7821	6" Lemon Dish	$1.25	$20

Notes

Notes

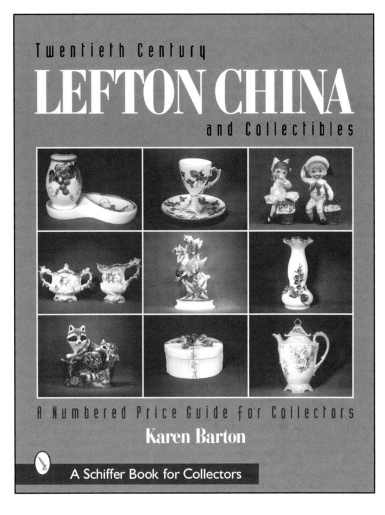

Twentieth Century Lefton China and Collectibles: A Numbered Price Guide for Collectors.
Karen Barton. This is the most comprehensive book written on Lefton China to date. What makes this book stand apart is the extensive price guide section containing company identification numbers, descriptions, and current prices for more than 7,600 different items made by the prolific Geo. Zoltan Lefton Company of Chicago, Illinois. Lefton collectors will also welcome the examples shown of over one hundred Lefton patterns, enabling quick identification of related pieces. A unique feature is the section describing and illustrating the popular Lefton Collections, including Colonial Village™, Historic American Lighthouses™, Li'l Country Folk™, Roadside U.S.A.™, and Tasha Tudor™ to name just a few. A company history, display of manufacturing marks, and over 360 color photographs of Lefton's figurines, boxes, plates, planters, teapots, vases, and more—including items never before published—round out this colorful and useful presentation.

Size: 8 1/2" x 11"   336 color photos   168 pp.
ISBN: 0-7643-1332-0   soft cover $29.95

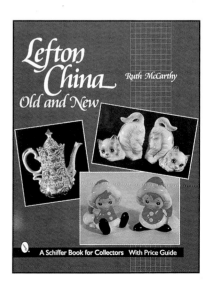